## Praise for *We Are All Addicts*

Dr. Carder Stout artfully deconstructs the meaning of addiction with the use of his own personal story, academic background in psychology, experiences with his patients, and thought provoking questions and exercises for the reader who may have never considered themselves an addict.

—Sarah Brokaw, *New York Times* bestselling author of *Fortytude: Making the Next Decades the Best Years of Your Life—through the 40s, 50s, and Beyond,* psychotherapist

The toxic guilt, crippling embarrassment, and vicious cycle of shame surrounding food addiction? Carder Stout gets it. It's like he can see me at three in the morning when I'm standing in front of the fridge (ravenous for what—to feel better about myself?). Thank you for writing *We Are All Addicts*. The advice about healing from within is spot on.

—Stephanie Laska, *USA TODAY* bestselling author, MEd, creator of *DIRTY, LAZY, KETO*

Dr. Carder Stout's latest writing adventure is a wonderful journey of recovery. This amazing book opens the reader's mind and offers a pathway to the healing soul. A book that will help any professional in the behavioral health field as well as anyone struggling with obsessive thoughts and compulsive actions.

—Dr. Ted Wiard EdD, LPCC, CGC, Founder of Golden Willow Retreat (an emotional healing center focused on grief and loss), Clinical Director Rio Grande Alcohol and Treatment Program

we are all
# ADDICTS

# we are all
# ADDICTS

**THE SOUL'S GUIDE TO KICKING YOUR COMPULSIONS**

## CARDER STOUT, PHD

Published in the United States by Viva Editions, an imprint of Start Midnight, LLC, 221 River Street, Ninth Floor, Hoboken, New Jersey 07030.

Printed in the United States
Cover design: Jennifer Do
Cover image: Shutterstock
Text design: Frank Wiedemann

First Edition.
10 9 8 7 6 5 4 3 2 1

Trade paper ISBN: 978-1-63228-081-7
E-book ISBN: 978-1-63228-138-8

*For Jennie, Maxine, and Sebastian.*
*You are my heart, my love, my soul.*

# CONTENTS

## Disclaimer:

The suggestions and recommendations made in this book are based on the author's knowledge, experience, and opinions. The methods described in this book are not intended to be a definitive set of instructions. Other methods and materials may accomplish the same end results. Results may vary.

There are no representations or warranties, express or implied, about the completeness, accuracy, or reliability of the information, products, services, or related materials contained in this book. The information is provided as is, to be used at your own risk.

This book is not intended as a substitute for consultation with a licensed health-care practitioner, such as your physician. Before you begin any health-care program or make lifestyle changes in any way, please consult a physician or another licensed health-care practitioner to ensure that you are in good health and that the examples contained in this book will not cause any harm. If you or someone you know is suffering from addiction, depression/other mental health issues, eating disorders, or the like, please seek initial medical attention.

Where appropriate, identities have been obscured out of concern for privacy.

# 1
# THE SOUL

There has been plenty of talk of the soul in recent years—and not where you would expect it. In his inaugural address in 2021, as he promised a bitterly divided nation that he would bring America together, President Joe Biden stated that his "whole soul is in it." He was quoting Abraham Lincoln's hallowed words after signing the Emancipation Proclamation in 1863, which gave those enslaved within the rebellious states freedom for the first time. In this context, is the soul synonymous with "heart" or "energy"? I guess we would have to ask President Biden to get the answer.

Walt Disney Pictures and Pixar Animation Studios released an animated film titled *Soul* at the end of 2020. It follows the journey of a musician who has been separated from his soul and finds his life bleak and uninspired without it. It also follows the musician's soul into "the Great Before"—the place where souls are taught their values before entering into someone's body. The film won the Academy Award for Best Animated Feature, and I understand why, beyond just the beauty of the film. To me, there is something oddly familiar about the story, perhaps a confirmation of an idea many of us hold: that there is something beyond this life, whatever it may be, that plays a role in shaping who we are. It is an ancient, archetypal story that has been passed from generation to generation since our earliest days. I wonder if this means that it's true.

Another beautiful film that stars souls is the 2021 Academy Award winner for Best Animated Short Film, *If Anything Happens I Love You*. In this short film, two grieving parents lose their daughter in a school shooting. The souls of the three family members attempt to heal them during this time of violent human tragedy, and ultimately they find peace. These souls are portrayed as conscious beings that show compassion, empathy, and love toward the humans they inhabit.

The soul is clearly in the zeitgeist right now. Not in a religious framework, mind you, but one of more universal appeal. When we hear about the soul, many of us nod our heads, even though we may not have our own specific understanding of what it is, exactly, or if we even have one. When I bring up the soul to my patients (which is quite often), the usual response is sheepishness or indecision, as if to say, *I know I should be paying more attention to this, but I'm not sure what to think.* When asked to give my opinion of the soul, I do so with enthusiasm and confidence. I believe that my opinion is more of a *knowing*—an intuitive and decisive point of view honed by years of inquiry and examination. You see, the entire foundation of my spiritual practice is that my soul is real. It is not an animated character, a hyperbolic concept, or some bit of dogma, but an intelligent, conscious entity that resides within me. (And, by the way, I get this information directly from my soul. I am not making this up.)

Yes, I speak with my soul every day—multiple times per day, actually. And my soul speaks back to me. No, I am not delusional; I am simply listening deep within for a response. My soul communicates in the form of thoughts, feelings, inspired moments, intuitive perceptions, passionate energy, images in my mind, dreams, and compassion. Without this relationship, I would be a very different person—still lost, perhaps. Much of my life, prior to connecting with my soul, can be summed up as a whirlwind of confused, negative, and self-destructive patterns. My years were filled with criticism and resentment, as I believed that the world owed me something and no one was there to guide me through it. But now I realize that my guide was always there. I had just turned my back on it—primarily because I doubted its existence. And when I found it again, everything changed.

Swiss psychiatrist and psychoanalyst Carl Jung (1875–1961) was arguably one of the most important figures in modern-day psychology. In his seminal writings, Jung devoted much of his time to explaining the soul. He believed that the soul was a conscious element in our psyche that promoted healing and offered direction. In therapy, he focused on attempting to decipher the will of the soul and how to determine its voice. Jung stated, "Learn your theories as well as you can, but put them aside when you touch the miracle of the living soul."[1] For Jung, the soul was the center of wisdom and truth, and communing with it was the most effective way to find happiness. I credit my most transformative psychological growth to the recognition of my soul's benevolent purpose.

Your soul is with you, always. From the moment you are born until the moment you die, the soul is wrapped around the core of your being. You come into the world without any separation between your soul and your mind. You are pure soul, a ball of love, a bundle of concentrated purity that is not yet disconnected from the grief of being human. The soul is pure consciousness untethered to human experience. It is our essence undiluted or altered by the experiences we have as humans. Unfortunately, as we mature and develop our cognitive function, this state of being is lost. Most of us forget these primal moments of peace as we navigate the complications of a busy world. When we feel emotional pain for the first time and doubt creeps

---

1    Jung, C. G. *Contribution to Analytical Psychology*. United Kingdom: Read Books, 2008, 361.

into our emerging psyche, our relationship with the soul begins to fray. It continues to unravel throughout our lives, because Planet Earth is no utopia and fear is an inescapable part of the human experience. It is mostly fear that fuels the counterpoint to the soul: the ego.

The ego is formed through the distillation of our lived experience, most of it challenging and difficult, as a protective mechanism to ward off anything perceived as dangerous. There are many definitions of the ego out there. For the purposes of this book, the ego is the lens through which we see ourselves and make sense of others we encounter along the way. It is a compilation of the many ways we feel about ourselves. It is an amalgamation of our thoughts, feelings, and experiences throughout life and the determinations we embody according to them. It is where we store our insecurity, judgment, anger, and confusion, which are fed by the interactions we have and the information we consume. The ego houses intergenerational trauma—pain that our parents, our parents' parents, and others through our ancestry have left unprocessed or unresolved and passed to us, whether by familial conflict, communication breakdowns, parental warmth or lack thereof, and so on.[2] Groups that were historically brutalized, subjugated, or marginalized by

---

2    Florien Meulewaeter, Sarah S. De Pauw, and Wouter Vanderplasschen, "Mothering, Substance Use Disorders and Intergenerational Trauma Transmission: An Attachment-Based Perspective," *Frontiers in Psychiatry* 10 (2019), https://doi.org/10.3389/fpsyt.2019.00728.

more dominant groups tend to have a higher incidence of intergenerational trauma, which leads to higher rates of addiction through the generations. Examples of these groups include African Americans in the United States who were subjected to enslavement, Native Americans who endured forced assimilation or annihilation, and those throughout the world who encountered colonization.[3] Parents who were abused or traumatized may also pass an emotional burden to their children, so intergenerational trauma can start at any point in a family history.

Even when we attempt to put the heavy weight of the past aside, when we look around the world and recognize the human suffering taking place—including the amount of fighting still required to achieve basic human and civil rights for all—it seems only natural that the ego becomes jaded with negativity and mistrust. The ego is a direct product of the pain we encounter. The consternations of survival overwhelm us and disrupt our communication with the soul. Ego consciousness is present in all human beings, and for the most part, we are unaware that it exists. Most of us are an embodiment of ego and no longer function with the soul as our guide, and because of this we are in a constant state of regression. This may be remedied by a simple reminder of what you already know.

---

3    Veronica L. Holyfield, "Addiction in the Context of Intergenerational Trauma," *Treatment Magazine*, October 4, 2021, https://treatmentmagazine. com/addiction-in-the-context-of-intergenerational-trauma/.

The soul is your biggest asset. It is the most powerful healing apparatus that exists. In fact, its very structure is created to mend what is broken in you. Psychologically, there is nothing that the soul cannot fix. Its primary function is to help you grow, evolve, and realize your most potent and actualized self. It is your greatest teacher and your most enthusiastic cheerleader that perpetually forgives you for your flaws and misdeeds. It is playful, creative, warm, and decisive. It will never recede or falter, as it is reinforced by the divine laws of the universe. I have heard people say, "My soul is damaged; my soul is broken; I need to heal my soul; my soul is suffering." In actuality, the soul is the most resolute of all our parts. It knows no suffering or pain and can never be damaged. The soul is aware that the ego is fragile and often wounded by the tribulations of the human experiment. It offers itself as a healer, if only we ask, if only we offer it recognition. The soul appreciates recognition—not in the sense that it asks for praise or validation, but that it becomes most active when we acknowledge its presence. This is an easy thing to do.

We have soul moments every day, even if we are not aware of them. Each time we look at something beautiful and are moved by its exquisite nature, we are connecting with the soul. During these instances of appreciation, give a brief nod to the soul—perhaps a simple thank-you. When you spend time with your children, your friends, or your family and there is laughter, gratitude, and authenticity, you are having a soul moment. Take a minute to reflect that glow back to the soul. When you feel your curiosity abounding and your mind expanding with thoughts of self-assurance and humility, your soul is present. Give your soul a quick hello. Improving your relationship with the soul, and sparking and continuing a dialogue with it, will fill you with a sense of belonging. As with anything else, if you incorporate this into your daily rituals, it will soon become a habit. Taking stock of these soul moments will help you become aware of how different they are from the ego moments. One springs from a nucleus of love, and the other from self-centered fear. Which do you prefer?

So why do so many refuse to acknowledge the soul's existence, even as we reference it in common language all the time? Jung wrote, "People will do anything, no matter how absurd, in order to avoid facing their own souls. They will practice Indian yoga and all its exercises, observe a strict regimen of diet, learn the literature of the whole world—all because they cannot get on with themselves and have not the slightest faith that anything useful could ever come out of their own souls."[4] Because the ego is so dominant, it attempts to negate the existence of the soul in a competitive power grab. It tries to convince us that the soul is a figment of our imagination. Our ego tells us that we must ignore

---

4    Jung, C. G. *Psychology and Alchemy.* United Kingdom: Taylor & Francis, 2014, 41.

our pain and rely on the mind to move rationally beyond our frailty. Unfortunately, the mind is not built with a healing function, and therefore we end up frustrated at our ineptitude at solving our own problems. Most of us have never even considered that we possess the ability to heal ourselves. Take a leap of faith with me: for a moment, choose to believe that the soul is real and has the ability to make your life infinitely better. Listen deeply. There is a voice inside you that is waiting for your acknowledgment. You may be surprised by what you hear.

You might find it curious that I am placing so much emphasis on the soul in a book about healing addiction. Maybe you find it naive to think that your addictions could be cured by fostering a relationship with the soul. Skepticism is a part of human nature, but it is expressly derived from the ego. The soul is grounded in a more optimistic point of view. I am a recovering addict. I have tried multiple different ways to address my obsessive thoughts and compulsive actions. I have endured several stints in rehabs, completed eons of therapy, and attended hundreds of twelve-step meetings. I am an expert in the field of addiction—living it, treating it, writing about it. I have found that of all the resources available to me, my own are the most effective. Nurturing a relationship with my soul has removed all the self-destructive thoughts and tendencies from my psyche. Although other methods helped nudge me along the way, it was the development of my own spiritual practice that eliminated addiction from my mind and body.

The idea of a spiritual practice is nothing new when it comes to addiction. In fact, many people who have achieved long-term sobriety swear by it. The most widely accepted of these are the twelve-step programs offered in almost every city across the globe. These unique fellowships and meetings cover several different types of addiction—alcohol, drugs, gambling, eating disorders, and codependency, to name a few.

Recovering addicts gather in church basements, community centers, and private homes to tell their stories and listen to others'. The camaraderie shared among twelve-step members is extremely valuable; feeling supported and understood by others with similar stories helps people feel accepted. This was my experience in Alcoholics Anonymous. That's where I made my friends—new friends who were also trying to decrease their appetite for substances. They became the backbone of my early recovery, and I continue to advocate joining a group of like-minded individuals to counter the tendency to isolate that is so prevalent with addicts. Yes, people help, there is no denying this—however, other parts of the program were harder for me to digest.

The twelve-step programs are essentially about God. The term *Higher Power* is used to ease folks into the concept without challenging their religious beliefs. God is all over the pages of twelve-step literature and promoted as the quintessential remedy for addiction.[5] The programs tell you to turn to God and ask him to remove your character defects, fears, resentments, and addictions—similar to the tenets of religions that encourage you to ask for atonement. The idea is that God will swipe away these things in a divine gesture, leaving you without addiction, anxiety, and anger. This will only happen, though, if you complete all twelve steps and continue to pass on the specific message of recovery to others.

Alcoholics Anonymous asks you to surrender to God, to turn your life and will over to this Higher Power, and to trust that this omnipotent being will solve your problems for you. From a psychological perspective, I have issues with this premise. I believe that promoting the notion that we should search for something outside ourselves to mend our brokenness is like carrying a false flag into battle. Many in Alcoholics Anonymous maintain that their program is the only way to success-fully combat addiction. They preach the efficacy of the twelve steps and warn that failing to comply will end in relapse. They are conditioned to believe—out of fear, mostly—that if they do not maintain strict adherence to the principles of the program, they are doomed to fail.

I have evidence to the contrary. I would never argue that there is only one path toward long-term

---

5   Alcoholics Anonymous World Services, *Twelve Steps and Twelve Traditions* (New York: Alcoholics Anonymous World Services, Incorporated, 2002).

sobriety. This would be a shortsighted and ego-minded perspective that would put limitations on other potential solutions. I am happy for those who have found success in these programs and have no judgment or criticism of them. I know that the twelve steps have been helpful to millions of people, but I found another solution that is more universally applicable and easily accessible to all of us.

My therapeutic work with patients centers on the theory that we have the inner resources, strength, and wisdom to resolve our own issues. Though sometimes we need assistance in rediscovering our internal fortitude, it is always in there. Primarily, that is my aim with this book—to remind you of something you already know but have forgotten along the way. That you possess everything you need to disrupt the addictive cycles inside your mind without necessarily putting blind faith in God. Your soul *is* your highest power—no need to search elsewhere. Instead of looking outward, it requires looking inward. Instead of relying on someone else to relieve our suffering, we use the healing mechanisms that we were born with. When you begin to differentiate the voice of your soul from that of your ego, you will understand what I mean.

Most of us cannot determine the difference between ego identification and the will of the soul. We vacillate between these two states of being throughout our lives. As we grow accustomed to our patterns of thinking, we believe them, even if they are rooted in negativity and fear. These thought patterns grow harder to overcome until we don't realize how much they're dominating our sense of self. But it doesn't have to be this way. You have simply given in to the onslaught of the ego. It tells us stories that are not true and steers our thoughts toward self-centered dissatisfaction. Here is a simple exercise to distinguish the two different voices—one from the ego, the other emanating from the soul.

## Exercise

*Type out or write down any anxious, critical, or resentful thought that you cannot seem to shake. For example, I WILL NEVER GET THAT JOB BECAUSE I'M NOT SMART ENOUGH. Look at this statement for a few seconds. See it for what it is: an old narrative that needs replacing. This is your ego filling you with doubt. Now, cross out or erase that statement from your screen and type out the exact opposite: I WILL ABSOLUTELY GET THAT JOB BECAUSE I'M SMART AND QUALIFIED. This is the statement coming from your soul, and it is the truthful one. Even if you don't end up getting hired, this is the message that your soul wants you to hear. It is the loving, optimistic, and accurate one. Do you feel the difference?*

*Type out five different negative thoughts that have been following you around for a while. Look at them and know they need replacing; do so with their exact opposite.*

You should now have a clear understanding of the different voices of the ego and the soul. I will outline various ways to communicate with your soul in the following chapters. Soon it will become second nature. When we are aligned with the soul, our obsessive thoughts will dissipate and judgment will subside. Addiction lives in the ego and is nowhere to be found in the soul. Identifying with the voice of the soul is the beginning of your journey toward freedom from addiction.

This journey will look different for everyone, and unfortunately, access to external support—be it from a friend, family members, a therapist, a medical doctor, or the authorities—varies widely for individuals in this country and this world. Your soul, however, is yours alone; it is at the ready to help you to heal and break your addictive cycles from within. Addressing the many cultural, institutional, and systemic failures of our society is outside the scope of this book—but could you imagine what the world would be like if every person, from the youngest child to the most powerful adult, allowed their soul to guide them?

# 2 | ADDICTION IS AN ARCHETYPE

**M**y mother drank vodka every morning. She would spike her orange juice with it as if it were perfectly normal. For many years in my childhood, I thought it was. My mother drank from the moment she got up to the moment she went to bed—always with that same glass in her hand. She could never shake her thirst for alcohol. She died of acute ethanol poisoning on the stairs at age sixty-six while bringing a drink up to bed. The addiction took her, and there was nothing I could do about it.

Her mother (my grandmother) was on oxygen for the last years of her life. When I visited her, she would lie in her bed chain-smoking Carlton cigarettes. I would light them for her when she asked. Every time she exhaled, she would say, "I've got to quit these damn things." Her prolonged smoking was a contributing factor to her death.

I am not trying to be morbid here. There were plenty of wonderful moments I shared with them as well—so much laughter and joy. That is what I remember most—their wonderful senses of humor, not the addiction. They were the matriarchs of my family, and I have nothing but love for them. But it occurred to me early on that I might be susceptible to developing or falling victim to an addiction myself. I read somewhere that addiction was thought to be hereditary, although this was just a theory.[6] It seemed true in my case, but I wasn't sure. I'd heard about a few twin studies done by prominent psychologists that targeted the question of nature vs. nurture.[7] Was addiction passed on from grandmother to mother and mother to son, or was it simply a product of the environment? The studies leaned toward the notion that addiction was hereditary, and that has been the predominant theory during my lifetime.

---

6 According to the American Addiction Centers' Rehab Guide, a family history of addiction does not necessarily mean that addiction resides within an individual. Supposedly, genes only account for about 50 percent of a person's risk of addiction. Other factors, such as easy access to addictive substances on a regular basis and other environmental influences, contribute to the possibility of addiction.

Mosel, Stacy. "Is Drug Addiction Genetic?" Edited by Wendy Manwarren Generes, February 8, 2022. https://americanaddictioncenters.org/rehab-guide/addiction-genetic.

7 Robert Weiss, "Nature, Nurture, and Addiction," *Psychology Today* (Sussex Publishers, LLC, November 30, 2020), https://www.psychologytoday.com/us/blog/love-and-sex-in-the-digital-age/202011/nature-nurture-and-addiction.

So, I grew up feeling as though I had a target on my back. It wasn't so much *if* the addiction was going to find me, but *when*. And when it did, it hit me like a freight train. I experienced addiction in many of its forms: food, sex, love, drugs, alcohol, fame, anger, and cigarettes, for starters. There was a certain amount of resentment I felt toward my ancestors for passing on an illness that filled me with a desire to want more of *every-thing*. I felt cursed and swore at them under my breath. I blamed them for my misfortune, and, as a result, for many years I remained angry.

Addiction followed me for decades and eventually brought me to my knees. After several years of therapy, I discovered a way to remain sober, a process that I will share in the pages that follow. At age thirty-four, I went to graduate school and studied for the next ten years to become a psychologist. All the while I thought about my addiction and marveled that it was no longer present. I have worked with hundreds of addicts since then both in residential treatment and in my private practice. I began to see commonalities in all of them. I realized that addiction would often come and go like the wind through the trees—that it is impermanent. Much like emotions of sadness or worry, addiction has the ability to shift, recede, and ultimately fade away. So I came to the conclusion that addiction was not part of my gene pool or DNA, as I had been led to believe. It is something far simpler than that—I realized that addiction is simply pent-up emotional energy.

What came as a surprise to me while working with

patients who did not identify as addicts was that most of them seemed to possess this same energy. They were not the typical addicts who struggled with alcohol or drugs, but they had other obsessions that kept them awake at night. They obsessed about work, their partners, their bodies, money, and trying to maintain a youthful appearance. They adopted patterns of unhealthy behavior according to their obsessive thinking, just like the addicts I had worked with in treatment. As I listened to all sorts of stories for many years, it became clear that this addictive energy was a link that connected them. Addiction looked far less like an illness and more like a universal tendency that everyone participated in. So, I came to the conclusion that addiction is an archetype.

*Archetype* is one of those words we've all heard but have a hard time putting our finger on, because we *almost* know its meaning—like *penultimate* or *ethereal*. We slip these words into sentences that don't really make sense, hoping that no one will catch us in our intellectual presumptions. We do it all the time: use slang, colloquialisms, and words that are out of context, and that's okay—conversations are usually less than perfect. In fact, we do it so much that it's pretty much an archetypal pattern. Yes, archetypes are alive and well—thriving all around us. You are engaged with several archetypes right now.

So, what does it mean, really?

Maybe it is best to start with an example. You are having one of those days when nothing goes right. You hit snooze a few too many times, and you're late. You burn your finger on the toaster, and there's no more milk in the fridge, so the coffee you usually enjoy tastes bitter and lifeless. There is construction on the highway, so you sit motionless, listening to bleak morning radio that lowers your mood even more. As soon as you walk into your workplace, a colleague looks at the expression on your face and says, "Looks like you're having one of those mornings." You simply nod your head and shuffle to your cubicle.

So, how did they know? Because they have had a morning just like yours. We all have. (One morning I was rushing so fast that I forgot to put my pants on. I drove away from my house in boxer shorts.) The experiences we all share and relate to are archetypal. They connect us to others as things we have in common, often mutually understood with a nod or a shrug or a smile. It's hard to quantify the vast scope of our archetypal interactions. Archetypes are working in your life right now. They shape our thoughts, our actions, our moods, and our sense of who we are. And they are as old as the hills.

Jung was the first to write about archetypes and referred to them as "forms or images of a collective nature that appear practically all over the earth."[8] Jung analyzed thousands of dreams during his career and found that people from all over the world were dreaming about the same myths, images, and ideas. He believed that there is a vast well of information where the

---

8   Jung, Carl Gustav. *Psychology and Religion.* United States: Yale University Press, 1960, 63.

history of all things is stored. He named it the *collective unconscious.*[9] The information in the collective unconscious is shared by everyone and perpetuates a sense of connectivity with all living creatures. According to Jung, the collective unconscious is also the resting place for archetypes. These archetypes show up at different times in our lives and provide us with an opportunity to grow and evolve.

Archetypes are patterns of thought, feelings, actions, and beliefs that we all have in common. They are the energy behind our most basic instincts, the voice behind our intuition, and the guiding principles behind the choices we make. Jung hypothesized that archetypes are "patterns of instinctual behavior" that guide the stories of our lives.[10] I have heard it said that every story has roots in an older story from our history. I don't mean that the specifics of your life are not vital and unique, but more that the foundation supporting them is bigger than just you, and it is shared by everyone—including all those who came before you. We have all suffered and lost people we love. We have all known great joy and witnessed the heroic deeds of others. We have all made mistakes, lied, and deceived people we care about. Each one of us knows what it feels like to be left out,

9   Jung, Carl Gustav. *The Archetypes and the Collective Unconscious.* United Kingdom: Princeton University Press, 1969.

10  Jung, Carl Gustav. *The Archetypes and the Collective Unconscious,* 44.

abandoned, and shunned. And we are united in the pain of getting our hearts broken. Although we may not look alike, the emotions we share bind us together like colorful leaves on a great big tree.

Infants fortunate enough to be born into caring families enter this world knowing they are loved. They gaze into the eyes of their parents and caretakers as they hold them and feed them and keep them safe. But as they grow, inevitably their needs are not always met, and they feel frightened and alone. Even a matter of minutes without the attention they crave leaves an impact on their fragile, emerging psyche. This is when they are first introduced to fear. They don't like the feeling, but they understand it, because they experienced the fears their mothers felt while they were in the womb. It was passed into their DNA, just like the immune system that keeps them healthy. So they grow up with this faint recollection of things, many of them unconscious but essential and powerful nonetheless.

As children, we constantly grapple with the distinction between right and wrong, but most of us already know the difference. We may hit or kick someone else, or we are mean, even cruel, but we understand that hurting someone is not okay, and we take no pleasure in the suffering of others. Most of us feel compassion, and we would rather save life than destroy it. If a bird stumbles around the backyard with a broken wing, our impulse is to help it, not break its other wing. If a friend is crying, we want to know why and offer a hug to soothe the pain. Before we are told these things, we have a deep sense of how to respond. We have archetypal wisdom guiding the principles that we live by, and it is stronger than the teachings we encounter every day.

As we grow up, we use all the resources available to muddle through life, attempting to find happiness. But most often, we feel something else, a combination of emotions, tumbling about like socks in the dryer. It's hard to sort them. Sometimes we feel stuck, repeating old patterns that no longer serve us. We know we shouldn't cheat on our significant others, but somehow we feel compelled to do so. Our doctor has strongly urged us to limit our sugar intake, but we sneak a family-size bag of gummy bears. We realize that our yelling disturbs the sanctity of the home, but in those moments, the anger we feel takes precedence.

It may sound simple to say that archetypes are patterns of behavior and thought, but in reality, they are incredibly complex. Archetypes have the ability to overtake our innate character and designate whom we become. And as they gain strength, we become powerless. We can take on an archetype's characteristics unwittingly—we do not even realize it is happening.

In my teen years, I got into a lot of trouble. I was experimenting with drugs on a fairly regular basis and had little regard for authority. I was kicked out of boarding school for lying to the headmaster, then scoffed at my downfall. I felt like a rebel—a rebel with something to prove. I wasn't quite sure what it was, but that didn't matter. During this time, I was overcome with energy that was different from my own. My parents said I was "going through a phase," and I don't disagree with them, but what was behind the phase? Certainly, it is not uncommon to be a rebellious teenager, but there was something else, something deeper. I understand now that I was possessed by an archetype.

When I bring up the idea of a rebel, perhaps an image of a famous actor like James Dean pops into your head, or even characters in literature such as Holden Caulfield of *The Catcher in the Rye*. You have definitely encountered a rebel somewhere on your life's journey, so there must be a feeling associated with that experience. You yourself probably felt rebellious, maybe as a teen against your parents or against your boss during an overwhelming urge to quit your job and move to Bali. We all share the story of the rebel, and each one of us can identify with it. So, a rebel is an archetype. It is not something we encounter all the time, but when we do, we instinctively know what it is.

The same could be said about the idea of God, a hero, a damsel in distress, or a villain. There are small amounts of these archetypes inside us, and sometimes one grows strong and takes over. And this comes at a price.

I'll go deeper into five universal archetypes: the Puella, the Victim, the Fighter, the Savior, and the Martyr.[11] As you read a brief summary of each, see if any resonate with you.

---

11 Stevens, Anthony in "The Archetypes" (Chapter 3). Ed. Papadopoulos, Renos. *The Handbook of Jungian Psychology: Theory, Practice and Applications.* United Kingdom: Taylor & Francis, 2012.

### The Puella (feminine) / Puer (masculine).

The Puella/Puer (Puer is the masculine) is the child in you that never wants to grow up. The Puella/Puer is fun-loving, audacious, and even derisive. People with strong Puella/Puer characteristics spend more time scribbling in books than they do reading them. They love to imagine themselves free from the restrictions of responsibility and daydream about the vast possibilities of life. However, as the Puella/Puer grows up, their immaturity often impedes their ability to develop in a healthy manner. At some point, they must choose between their child and adult selves—as traversing these two states creates only confusion, sadness, and an inability to find their true calling.[12]

### The Victim

To the Victim, the world is unfair. It is a place where they feel unwanted and their needs are either ignored or unwelcome. Victims expect to be mistreated, whether by their colleagues, their family, or society at large. Intuitively, they believe that they are unworthy of good things, but it still angers them when they are treated poorly. Victims are jealous of anyone they consider to be more fortunate. They seek a sympathetic ear—anyone who will listen, really—and enjoy gathering with other victims who reinforce their misery. Victims never take responsibility for their own misfortune but

---

12  Jung, Carl Gustav. *The Archetypes and the Collective Unconscious*, 158–159.

instead condemn others for creating it—blaming every-thing and everyone else.

### The Fighter

The Fighter archetype shows up in people who are defiant, passionate, and always have something to prove. Fighters are vocal about their point of view and support their cause with conviction and determi-nation. They are not afraid of conflict and will argue to get their point across, no matter the consequences. They will plead with you to join their ranks and use psychological warfare to persuade you if necessary. But underneath this façade, the fighter often feels lost and depressed. Still, you will never see one raise a white flag in defeat—just the opposite. No matter the odds, they will trudge through deep snow to reach the top of the mountain. And when they get there, there is a feeling of victory—for a brief instant.

### The Savior

The Savior archetype is present in people who are naturally kind and generous. Saviors are sympathetic toward those in crisis and often lose themselves in the lives of others. They will always put you first and believe that they are guided by the higher principles of compassion and justice. Saviors often have unresolved trauma in their psyche, and their dedication to others helps avoid the pain of attending to it. It's much easier to externalize their life's mission than to look inward and uncover their sadness. They make cheerful company, supportive partners, and reliable friends. But this happiness is fleeting, as it is only found through a sacrifice of their own needs.

## The Martyr

The Martyr archetype is found in those who are filled with devotion and fervor. Martyrs often take the road less traveled, as their beliefs are unconventional, unpopular, and usually in opposition to the establishment. Martyrs will stand next to you on the picket lines and are not afraid to voice their opinion from the pulpit. Martyrs are far from humble, and it is this lack of humility that causes their one-sided perspectives. Their hubris is often their downfall. There is nobility in the selfless nature of Martyrs, but their conviction is often overshadowed by emptiness and despair. Even in a crowd of people, the Martyr still feels alone.

Do any of these seem familiar? Do you see yourself in one of them, or maybe more than one? We ask ourselves, *why do I repeat these patterns over and over again? Why do I fight against authority?* or *why do I let people take advantage of me?* Archetypes can feel natural. *It's just who I am*, you may think. *What's wrong with that?*

But the truth is, these archetypes are not who you are at all. You are bigger, taller, and more intelligent than the archetypes that hold you captive. You are so many things—a multitude of strengths and contradictions, a product of your own vivid history, and a combination of soul and human being. You are diverse, distinctive, and wonderful down to the core. Most of the time, we don't even realize that our authentic nature has been hijacked because we are convinced that the archetype is who we really are. But you are not an archetype.

So why all this discussion about archetypes in a book about addiction? Well, for one simple reason: addiction is archetypal. It is something that *we all* know intimately. Not in the way you might expect, though. You may not think of yourself as an addict; neither do an overwhelming majority of people. You may know someone who claims to have an addictive personality or difficulty saying no. These are not addicts in the way that society currently perceives addiction. For as long as their overindulgence or tendency to want more does not have serious consequences, society gives them a pass.

We think of addicts as those addicted to alcohol and drugs, typically, and this belief is reinforced by a pervasive attitude in our homes, classrooms, and the world at large. But this is a limited and misleading understanding of the nature of addiction—one that curtails our ability to feel empathy, for one may struggle to have empathy for something they have not experienced. When someone is angry, we interpret their anger according to the anger we ourselves have felt. We have a framework in which to gauge its severity and a reference point derived from our own emotions. With addiction, most people dismiss it as an affliction far removed from themselves, something that is not relatable and difficult to understand. Nothing could be further from the truth. Addiction is archetypal and something that we all share.

It is an energy many of you are experiencing right now. This may be difficult for you to grasp, but it will become clearer as you continue to read. In order to revise our working definition of addiction, it is helpful to revisit the negative stereotypes we generally accept about it. Most of them are false.

## The Addict

We are raised hearing and internalizing the worst about addicts: that they are self-destructive and will do anything to get their fix, even if it puts themselves or others in harm's way. Addicts are manipulative, controlling, and dishonest. Addicts are needy and always seem to be asking for something—whether it's money, a ride, or your attention. Addicts are troubled, untrustworthy, and deviant. Maybe you know an uncle, a classmate, or a cousin who went to rehab—but not you, no way. Never. The addict is *someone else* who is struggling in a way that you can never understand. Push them away, these addicts—quarantine them so we are safe.

These common attitudes are wrong, dead wrong. These stereotypes are created by uninformed doctors, the media, and your gossipy neighbor. Yet we believe them, or at least part of us does, because we are usually afraid of things we don't understand.

Addiction is merely energy that flows through us at different points in our lives. For some, the energy becomes concentrated and stuck like water in a dam—but there is always a way to release it, and I'll spend the rest of the book discussing those ways. Because addiction doesn't just inhabit the stranger that lives next door; it's not something far in the distance that only affects *other people*. No, addiction is closer than that— closer than you think. Look into a mirror and you will see it. Yes, it is inside you. Inside you right now.

# 3 | A NEW UNDERSTANDING OF ADDICTION

Addiction is not a disease. Psychology types have been trying to convince you it is for the past fifty years, but this is false. Addiction does not grow in the body like a virus or attack your cells like an autoimmune disorder. It is not like a bum kidney that requires dialysis or a weakened heart that needs replacing. No, addiction is far less imposing than any of these afflictions.[13]

Let's face it: one can argue that the most seasoned and qualified professionals in the world, with all their PhDs, MDs, and advanced degrees, have been doing a terrible job at not only treating addiction, but under-

---

13 John Davies (2018) "Addiction is not a brain disease," *Addiction Research & Theory*, 26:1, 1–2, DOI: 10.1080/16066359.2017.1321741

standing it as well. The number of drug overdoses increases with every year, and global suffering is profound.[14] We call it a crisis here in America, and I would agree with that, but the crisis stems from our inability to change how we treat it. Addiction is looked at as a plague, a scourge, a nightmare. Society portrays it as a boogeyman—*don't let it get you!* I assure you it's not. It is bound to get you at some point, I can also assure you of that. But it's not what you think. It is much more manageable. My professional method does not require years of twelve-step meetings, complete abstinence, or twenty-eight days of inpatient treatment. It will simply require you to think a bit differently. And with this newfound perspective, you will release it for good. That is exactly what I did.

In my first thirty-five years on earth, I fought a prolonged battle with addictive cycles. You could say that I was addicted to almost everything. I craved sugar as a young boy. I would steal candy bars from the local convenience store when I was out of money. At night, I would sneak downstairs and eat pints of ice cream while my parents slept. I dreamed of Pepperidge Farm cookies and would hide bags of them under my bed. The sugar gave me a rush, and I liked the feeling. I had

---

14  Recent data from the CDC's National Center for Health Statistics suggests that the drug overdose death toll in the United States has increased by about 28.5 percent since the previous year (2021). "Drug Overdose Deaths in the U.S. Top 100,000 Annually." Centers for Disease Control and Prevention, November 17, 2021. National Center for Health Statistics. https://www.cdc.gov/nchs/pressroom/nchs_press_releases/2021/20211117.htm.

far more energy to play. But when the effects wore off, I felt dull and tired—until I consumed some more. And so the cycle continued.

My food addictions continued into my teen years, when I began to experiment with disordered eating. At first, I restricted my food intake until I reached a desired physical appearance. Soon, I discovered that if I consumed a large amount of food and then purged it, a feeling of euphoria would pulsate through my brain and body. I became hopelessly bulimic after that, and my relationship with food took a dangerous turn. I began to obsess about it constantly, with thoughts of how much I was eating and when I should release the food from my body. Within a matter of months, I was malnourished, depressed, and anxious.

You see, I was overtaken by these obsessive thoughts about food. I couldn't stop thinking about it in all its forms. The only thing that would stop my thoughts was engaging in a compulsive act: the purge. After I emptied my stomach, the thoughts would clear, and I would feel at peace. That is, until the cycle began to repeat itself.

That is the essence of addiction. Addiction is a cluster of obsessive thoughts followed by compulsive actions. An addictive cycle is when this pattern continues and begins to dominate your life. When we are caught in the throes of an addictive cycle, we cannot escape from this loop of obsession and compulsion. It is like a perfect circle that perpetually chases its tail. All of us have been swept up in this loop. Let's take a look at another example: let's talk about love.

Do you remember the feeling when a crush begins? Maybe there was something strangely intriguing about someone in your class at school. You may have caught yourself staring a few times before glancing away. That person, who was making you feel funny down to your toes, would start creeping into your thoughts when you were back at home. The thoughts would not go away— they plagued you, but in a benevolent sort of way, until you saw that person in the flesh again. Then the thoughts seemed to subside, and you could finally focus on something else. This was the energy of addiction introducing itself at an early age.

And then you began to talk on a regular basis, texting on your phone as a way to communicate. You came to rely on these pleasant exchanges for validation and a sense of belonging. Your texts were always answered within a few minutes, as you knew your crush was always within striking distance of the phone. You texted, and a response came. This arrangement worked perfectly—until it didn't. One day you sent a text, and nothing came back. That's strange. Maybe it went into the ether, so you texted again. Still no response. Now you were a bit worried, and annoyed, constantly peering at your phone. Your thoughts ramped up in a frenzy—*Am I being ignored? Did I do something wrong? Are they mad at me? Am I being too needy? Are they breaking up with me?* You checked your phone compulsively for the next few hours and finally, a reply: "Sorry, I was in a movie and had my phone on silent."

All that needless suffering—does it sound familiar?

It should, because it is archetypal. We have all had a situation like this in our past. These phones we carry in our pockets are certainly handy for staying connected, but they are also a perfect way for addictive energy to seep in through the cracks in our psyche. The moment we get a text back, the addictive cycle is interrupted, and we exhale a big sigh of relief. We are able to relax for a moment—the world is not caving in. We restore our balance until the next time it happens. And believe me, it will. This is all addiction is—obsessive thoughts followed by compulsive behavior. It is probably visiting your life today.

Addiction is not something that is inside you, but rather an external force that moves through us with regularity. You are not born with addiction in your blood. It is not part of your DNA strands and is not passed on to you by a parent or relative.[15] Addiction is something completely separate from you, and as long as you treat it this way, it cannot hurt you. The energy of addiction creates a disturbance in your mind that leads to repetitive and confusing behaviors. It is not like any other energy we encounter in the complex web of human experience. It has a mind of its own and will attempt to sway you with a powerful surge of redirection. It is playful, intelligent, convincing, and purposeful. When

---

15  Mosel, Stacy. "Is Drug Addiction Genetic?" Edited by Wendy Manwarren Generes, February 8, 2022. https://americanaddictioncenters.org/rehab-guide/addiction-genetic.

it shows up, there is an initial tingling of the senses. You may actually feel its presence in your mind, like a euphoric rush of warm air in your skull. It is unmistakable if you know what you're looking for, and if you don't, I will show you how to spot it.

Now, when I say *energy of addiction*, I am referring to the archetypal energy that flows through the universe. It is not yours to keep, although many of us hold on to it for a while. Just like all archetypes, this energy finds us at certain times in our lives, at certain moments. Usually, it infiltrates us when we are feeling insecure or distracted. It slips in like the wind under the door. It takes up residence in our unconscious mind, slowly transforming into conscious thoughts. But archetypal energy is not who you are at all. It belongs to the world and to all those who have come before you. You share it with everyone, but when it's present in you, you feel like it's yours. This is fairly egocentric thinking, right? You are not the only person to have ever felt this way, not by a long shot.

We humans often feel sad. We wake up sometimes and just feel blue. This feeling may last for an hour, a day, a week. Perhaps we don't know what is causing it. Our friends notice our downtrodden mood and try to cheer us up. *Good luck.* We tell them that we are feeling "depressed." Many of us use the word *depressed* in common language when we actually mean sad. There is a marked difference between clinical depression and sadness[16]—clinical depression usually stems from chemical imbalances in the brain, while sadness derives from the inevitable circumstances of our lives. And when we bring it up, our friends often respond by telling us what they do when they are feeling the same way— because we have all felt melancholy at some point. Irritable, tired, fed up, and sad. But we are not this sad feeling that consumes us. Far from it. It will inevitably leave us, and our mood will shift.

The same goes with anger. It sneaks up on us like a cat pouncing from behind a bush. The energy is so inflated, so powerful, that it overtakes our senses and our better judgment. We howl and roar and stomp and slam with reckless abandon. How is it possible to go from feeling serene one moment to profoundly agitated the next? Well, anger, just like sadness, is simply energy. It overtakes you in moments of weakness, when you were looking the other way. But you are not anger— you are merely expressing the archetypal anger that is flowing through you. And when you release it, this energy heads off and reconnects with an infinite number of angry atoms swirling through the air.

When we are feeling sad or angry, we are overtaken

---

16 According to the National Institute of Mental Health (NIMH), depression (major depressive disorder or clinical depression) is "a common but serious mood disorder. It causes severe symptoms that affect how you feel, think, and handle daily activities, such as sleeping, eating, or working. To be diagnosed with depression, the symptoms must be present for at least two weeks." National Institute of Mental Health. "Depression." National Institute of Mental Health. U.S. Department of Health and Human Services, 2018. https://www.nimh.nih.gov/health/topics/depression.

by the will of the ego. We know these feelings, as the ego has been dominant for most of our lives. And when we are in the vortex of negative emotions, we succumb to them and allow them to run their course. But they are not ours to keep, and a simple acknowledgment of the soul's presence will hasten their departure by altering our state of mind almost immediately. Sadness and anger are ego moments. Joy and patience are soul moments. So how do we move from ego to soul? Remember, it all starts with a belief that it's possible. Ask for your soul to help you out. Speak with it, and I guarantee it will respond.

We single addiction out as if it doesn't belong with our other emotions. But addiction is no different. In all my years as an addict and the fifteen years I have treated addicts, I have never heard anyone say, "I'm feeling addicted." We use the phrases *I'm feeling angry* or *I'm feeling sad* quite readily. We understand what they mean. But the way we speak about addiction is vastly different. First of all, we would most likely think that this person was referring to drugs or alcohol, because we are conditioned to believe that is what addiction means. But considering addiction to be a universal frequency that infiltrates all our minds and manipulates our actions, it doesn't have to be drugs or alcohol. It is ubiquitous, and no one is exempt. The addictive cycle will find us one way or another. It happens through love, sex, anger, fame, vanity, the future, exercise, food, work, success, the past, fear, resentment, alcohol, drugs, phones, technology, exaggeration, lies, and so many other things.

Let's change the way we speak about addiction. The correct way to describe your state of mind when this energy is present is *I'm feeling obsessive right now* or *I'm feeling compulsive*. Does that make sense? It accurately delineates your pattern of thought. In a perfect world, there would be no judgment about the tendencies we have, but this world is far from that. Not only is *obsessive* a more precise way to convey your emotions, it is also a word that is more widely accepted and understood. Say your colleague says to you, "I'm totally obsessing about that promotion, and I've been working every weekend for months to get it." You might respond, "Well, that makes sense. I hope you get it." You empathize with his condition because you've been in a similar situation. You know what it feels like to obsess about something and to tailor your behavior to achieve a desired goal. There it is again—the loop of addictive energy. Obsession and compulsion—no more, no less. Carl Jung referred to psychological energy as "a cluster of energy in the unconscious, charged by historic events, reinforced through repetition, embodying a fragment of our personality, and generating a programmed response and an implicit set of expectations."[17] This is addiction in a nutshell.

Remember, the most important thing to keep in mind is that your addiction is a powerful entity that is separate from you. So, let's get more acquainted with it.

---

17 Hollis, James. *The Best of James Hollis: Wisdom for the Inner Journey.* United States: Chiron Publications, (n.d.), 112.

**Exercise**

*Close your eyes and think of your addiction as being alive. Imagine what it looks like. Perhaps it is a person, a group of fireflies, a roaring fire, or a cartoon character from your childhood. Remember, it is resting inside you, so spend some time pinpointing an image that feels right. When the figure has arrived, give your addiction a name. Something that suits it best. Begin by introducing yourself and ask if it would like to talk. Invite it over for coffee and conversation. During this initial meeting, begin to ask your addiction questions. Here are a few:*

1. How long have you been with me?
2. Do you want to hurt me in some way?
3. What are you looking for, exactly?
4. Is there something that you want from me?
5. How can we become friends?

*Tell your addiction that you are no longer going to ignore it. Assure it that you will be more attentive and show it respect and love. Remind it that you're sharing the same space, for now. Be kind and compassionate. Spend five minutes a day speaking with your addiction. You will begin to understand it differently.*

You will be amazed that a small amount of recognition and positive attention will transform your relationship to addiction. This new attitude will entice your addiction to surrender and no longer control you. You may think that this seems counterintuitive—to love your addiction. I tell my patients constantly that a healthy psyche is one that accepts, respects, and even loves all the energy inside it. When the energy of addiction is inside you, it is not something to be feared. It has an agenda and wants to be heard. If you ignore it, it will continue to cause trouble until you are brought to your knees. It's asking for your recognition, and once you pay attention to it, much like a needy child, it will eventually calm down.

Another way to work with this potent energy is to disrupt its natural flow. When addiction is present, an incessant cycle of focused thoughts bounce around your head, until the compulsive act—taking that drink, checking that phone and seeing a reply—calm your mind. But there are many actions you can engage in that are healthier than these compulsive ones. There are alternatives to compulsion that will free you from this obsessive thinking as well. Remember, you have the ability to move from ego consciousness to an alignment with your soul through your thoughts and actions.

After I had successfully tamed the many forms the addictive energy had taken throughout my life, only one remained. When I was getting clean from drug and alcohol abuse, I picked up tobacco. This is not uncommon, to install another addiction when you are working tirelessly to stop another. Cigarettes became a shield for me to defend against the addictive energy of sex, food, chemicals, alcohol, vanity, and love. (Yes, I had them all, and I am not ashamed about it in the least.) But those cigarettes became a nuisance, and I wanted to give them up for good. That's when I began using the exercise of speaking to the energy. I imagined it was an ominous storm cloud that hovered over me. I spoke to it often, and the cravings began to cease. But I added an extra layer of protection on top of that. I know you will find it helpful.

When the thoughts returned—the thoughts that were urging me, pleading with me, begging me to drive to the store to buy a pack of blue American Spirits, I engaged them in conversation. What they told me made perfect sense. *Do something different*, they urged. *You have given us enough time and attention and that is what we asked for, so go your own way now.* You see, the consciousness of addiction didn't want to destroy me at all; it simply wanted validation. It needed to be heard and seen, and spoken to as anyone does. It wanted to be understood and embraced, and cared for just like we do. It was showing me a way to break the cycle, and I took its advice.

I began to carry three new items in my bag—a good book, a journal, and a photo of my family. Each time the whispers would return, I took my book out and began reading, which is something I love to do. Reading is an extension of the soul. In a matter of minutes, the whispers would cease. The next time they resurfaced, I took out the picture of my family and held it in my hand. How beautiful they all looked with those silly grins. Embracing family in person or through an image connects you to the soul. Then, I took out my journal and began to write. I wrote about my family and how much they mean to me. Writing positive words of appreciation is a direct conduit to the soul. Immediately, the whispers ceased again. It was like magic. I had replaced the compulsive acts with healthy ones, and I enjoyed the process of doing so. I could feel the addictive energy falling out of my mind and leaving my body. I was free.

There are so many forms of self-love. Anything you do for yourself that is healthy and spiritual is an act of self-love, which is the will of the soul. Don't get caught up in the word *spiritual*. The way I'm using it means anything that uplifts your spirit in a positive and healthy way. This spirituality is the essence of growth and evolution, and most of us engage with it daily. Every time we give someone a hug, tell someone we love them, look at something with gratitude, or expand our horizons, we are being spiritual and having a soul moment.

Some of the activities I cherish each week that have helped me immensely with addictive energy are going on hikes, walking my dogs at the beach, working out, eating healthy food, spending time with friends, playing with my children, taking baths, reading, journaling, laughing at myself and with others, doing yoga, meditating, praying, having conversations with my addiction storm cloud, sleeping well, appreciating what I have, enjoying this brief time on earth. Now you make a list, too. Your soul will thank you for it.

Addiction is not a death sentence—far from it. It

doesn't want to harm you or destroy your life; it simply wants your attention. When you start engaging with it regularly, speaking with it and asking it questions, you will see how obedient it becomes. When you are feeling its energy pulsing inside you, let someone know that you are "feeling obsessive" today. Let's change the language of addiction together to help everyone comprehend it in a new way. Right now, I am addiction-free. I know that your freedom is just around the corner. Believe me, it's possible.

In the chapters that follow, I will discuss various addictive loops that may be holding us back from our best selves (or worse). I encourage you to read each one, even if the specific addiction seems not to apply to you. Reading every chapter will offer you a full understanding of addictive energy and the most comprehensive discussion of the soul, as every reader can relate to the many anecdotes and benefit from the various exercises. The cumulative effect will be a new vision of yourself and those around you and an alignment with your soul that will help you heal the parts of yourself most in need.

Let's begin.

# 4 | VANITY AND FAME

**M**ost of us have a mirror hanging over our bathroom sink. When we wash our hands or brush our teeth, we are more apt to look at ourselves. Some of the time we smile into the reflection because we like what we see, but more often than not, we focus on something that we do not like. Perhaps there are bags under our eyes or our cheeks appear sunken. We sigh over the way our brow furrows and has left wrinkles on our forehead. Or the extra baggage we have on our hips that we try to smooth away. We are overly conscious of our looks, and this makes us self-critical. We judge our appearance from a place of dissatisfaction—and when we do so, we forget about what's inside.

As we grow from childhood into adolescence, we

become aware that how we look makes a difference. We cling to a pair of blue sneakers, ask for a certain type of haircut, and become more conscious of the color of our skin. Like all members of the animal kingdom, we are born with a biological preference for attractiveness. Think of birds displaying their plumage in a bid to attract a mate. What sets humans apart is how we define attractiveness—it tends to be cultural, rather than biological. We as a species are greatly influenced by those around us. In a sense, we are always competing, whether it is to fit in or to set ourselves apart. The way in which we perceive ourselves largely depends on the types of experiences we have had and the beliefs we have established according to them.

In our childhood, we glean much of our conception of what is attractive from our primary caregivers, whose ideals were also influenced by their parents, and so on. Every time we watch our mother apply makeup, we internalize the message. If our parents make a comment about their waistlines and the prospect of going on a diet, we take notice. If we had parents who were loving, kind, and psychologically healthy, there is a good chance we may have a positive sense of self. For people who do not have parents like this, their sense of self may be fractured. Either way, as kids we collect the details of their words and actions and store them in our psyche. A pro-beauty narrative is often reinforced by conversations with our classmates, what we see on TV or online, and the stories we read in books. Studies have shown that attractive people do tend to receive more opportunities, better treatment, and more advantages in general. In fairy tales, the tall handsome prince usually marries the beautiful princess. The overarching theme is simple: physical beauty and stature equate to happiness. I can tell you, from a psychological perspective, nothing could be further from the truth.

But we believe the fairy tale, for the most part. We buy into the myth, even if we think we don't, even if we know better. How could we not? It is everywhere. And as we grow older, we see it beaming from billboards, pinging from Instagram, blaring from TV ads, and photoshopped on the glossy pages of fashion magazines. We are led to believe that if we are tall, thin, youthful, wealthy, and successful, that somehow the hardships of life will magically disappear and we will be overcome with a sense of peace and fulfillment. The story is so enticing that we alter our natural patterns of thought and behavior in an attempt to attain it. But most of us fall short, and this leaves us feeling poorly about ourselves, as though we have failed. We are never satisfied, and the addictive loop begins.

Take weight as an example. While no one ever hears of falling into an addictive loop of obsessive thought and compulsive action around how intelligent we are, most people in Western civilization can relate to a preoccupation with how much we weigh. This can lead to an unhealthy relationship with food. We either love it too much or feel that it is barrier that prevents us from achieving our goals. It is a delicate dance we perform with food—restricting our consumption, giving up types we love, denying our urges, starving ourselves, constantly hopping on the scale. We judge ourselves by our garment size or the way we slide into a pair of jeans when these are in no way an indicator of who we are as individuals. Some of us—not all—place equal emphasis on the way we look and how we feel about ourselves. Unfortunately, the two have become so inextricably linked that it is often hard to tell which one is which— they are two sides of the same coin. In the struggle to parse this out, the ego is raging.

Remember, the ego is merely your own perception of you. It is the specific lens through which we interpret who we are and how we feel, and we tend to be a self-centered species. We look at our reflection constantly and ruminate on its state of affairs often. For many of us, the ego attaches itself to negative, harmful, and limiting beliefs. Incessant negative thoughts break down our defenses, and the energy of addiction slips in. When we feel emotionally vulnerable, the ego whispers to us that changing our physique—the compulsive action— will heal the wound. It does not. At the very most, it may pause the nagging, judgmental thoughts—until we notice something else that we don't like.

As such, looking younger is a big business. Some people do everything in their power to cover up bald spots and thinning hair. They wear hats, vigorously apply Rogaine, and receive hair-follicle transplants. New hair, they surmise, with somehow reduce their unhappiness. If only it were that simple. Some battle at any cost against the wrinkles on their faces with chemical injections, spa treatments, lasers, and night cream. When the lines are gone, they breathe a sigh of relief, until another one appears—and another always does. Many people I know do this on a regular basis, and I do not judge them for it, but I try to guide them toward their inner selves and reduce their focus on the external. Make no mistake about it, these pursuits are habit-forming and usually turn into addictive cycles. We are convinced that we will love ourselves when we look perfect, but we don't. Life doesn't work that way.

The self-obsession that accompanies our pursuit of perfection looks a lot like vanity. Vanity is the appearance of an infatuated and narcissistic sense of self, but this is usually on the surface. When someone is vain, it does not necessarily mean they have a high opinion of themselves. Often, the way someone behaves does not align with the way they feel about themselves. Most of my patients who are vain are also deeply insecure. Underneath the façade and self-aggrandizement, there is usually a psychological wound of feeling inferior. Perhaps it is better to seem vain than profoundly wounded. Vanity is the epitome of self-centeredness— one of the most prominent aspects of addiction.

When we look for our models of perfection, where do we find them? For many Americans, it is the world of celebrity. The stars of our screens, big and small, are role models, idols, and heroes to many of us. They are the performers, athletes, and influencers we love to watch. Most people imagine that the lives of celebrities are glamorous and wonderful. We dream of what it would be like to live in their shoes—those big mansions, the clothes, the special-edition sports cars, all that money. We hunger for it with such vigor that rarely do we spend a day without consuming some kind of celebrity gossip. The internet is bursting with it, and we click on the links, hoping for some insight that will deconstruct the mystery. But like the great Oz, who was merely an old man looming behind the curtain, the myth of fame is only a story without any foundation in truth.

What escapes the common sense of many is that celebrities are just regular people who have been elevated to a certain status. There is nothing special about them, really. They are ordinary people, often from humble beginnings, who have navigated their way upward in their industries through sheer luck and talent. I have treated many famous people in my psychology practice over the last decade. Each of them is uniquely wonderful—as are all my patients. But what sets them apart from my other clients is a belief in their own inadequacies. Not to say that only celebrities feel this way—it is not uncommon for humans to feel less than—but many of the ones I have treated seemed to be racked with a lack of self-confidence. Out in public they wear a mask of perfection—sparkly teeth, perfect hair, and rehearsed responses to media questions—but behind closed doors, they often shrink into fear, self-loathing, and sadness. The pressure to be perfect is immense. Something about being so high on a pedestal with all those eyes on them makes them feel unworthy. Most celebrities are not the people they pretend to be while in front of a crowd. This contradiction can be especially disruptive.

I worked for a few years with a movie star who had won all the awards—Oscar, Golden Globe, and Emmy, to name a few. They were a complex person who marched to the beat of their own drum. Every morning, they woke up in terrible fear—fear that their position as supreme would soon be taken away from them. They were never satisfied by the roles they were offered and believed that there was some industry-wide conspiracy to dethrone them. They had all the money they could ever need, but they remained at home most of the time, shrouded in the dim lights of their basement. Their relationships never lasted long, and their friends were scarce. They were lonely and confused and felt as though their life was meaningless. My work with them revolved around an excavation of the harmful beliefs about themself. Once we discovered them, we began to reshape them into more truthful and positive ones. Learning to love themself, not fame or fortune, was the key to their happiness.

So why do we compare our lifestyles to those of the rich and famous? Why do we obsess about what others have and we don't? Why do we believe that how we look is more important than how we feel? Well, I think it is caused by an aversion to dealing with the emotional pain of being human. Instead of looking inward to healing, we reach for something that distracts us from the confusion of our low self-esteem and emotional trauma. This is a well-known characteristic of addiction.

We avoid the problem by running away from it instead searching for a more immediate fix.

Unfortunately, our brokenness still remains after the quick fix wears off, and we are left in a similar or even more despondent state. Addiction fools us into believing that the addition of something new will soothe our restlessness, but we end up ignoring the actual source of our discomfort. Wouldn't it be great if you did not need to hide your wrinkles or cover up your bald spot? Wouldn't it be nice to not want to photoshop ourselves into perfection?

When we perceive ourselves in a negative way, we are living in our heads and not our hearts. We have become attached to our ego, not our soul. We are entrenched in our humanness and not our spirituality. Why is this important? Well, addiction tends to attach itself to our ego, while it is unable to penetrate the confines of our soul. You see, the soul is your essence. It is your authentic self. It is the stamp of divinity that resides in your heart. It is the real you the way you were born into the world. Your soul is generous and kind. It is loving, compassionate, expansive, and optimistic. It is your joy, your tenderness, and your curiosity. Your soul is your spiritual center that believes in growth and transformation. It is your intuition, your instinct, and your appreciation. When we are aligned with our soul, there is no room for negativity or judgment. Your soul will defend you from everything that is not natural to who you are, authentically, allowing you to ignore whatever false standards the ego may tout. Addiction is nowhere in sight.

It may be a novel idea to heal our addictions through the soul, but I am living proof that it works. When we become soul-aligned, we seal the cracks in our psyche that addiction tends to move through. Instead of flowing through us, the energy of addiction swirls around us, recedes, and dissipates. The soul is an impenetrable fortress of good. It has our best interests in mind and always maintains balance and psychological health. In most of us, it is buried underneath layers of emotional trauma, negative thinking, and fear. But it is there, nonetheless. The soul appreciates when we acknowledge its presence. The more you build your relationship with your soul, the more it will rise into consciousness and defend you from harmful thoughts and behaviors.

I have developed an exercise to help you connect deeply to your soul. If you do this each morning, you will feel a profound shift in how you view the world. You will feel energized, positive, and free from old negative thoughts. The soul wants you to grow, laugh, enjoy your life, and be filled with love—aligning with it will help you achieve this.

## Exercise
### Connecting to the Soul
*When you get up in the morning, find a quiet place. This will be a fifteen-minute exercise, so make sure it's a secluded spot where no one will interrupt you. Turn off your phone and be present with the experience.*

## WE ARE ALL ADDICTS

*Repeat these words:*

> *I call out to the most authentic voice inside me, the voice of my soul.*
> *I ask you, my soul, to connect deeply with me.*
> *I ask you, my soul, to be present with me today and tonight in all things I do.*
> *I ask you, my soul, to make your presence known to me.*
> *I ask you, my soul, to fill me with your love and beauty.*
> *I ask you, my soul, to fill me with your kindness and light.*
> *I ask you, my soul, to fill me with your energy and warmth.*
> *I ask you, my soul, to fill me with your calmness and serenity.*
> *I ask you, my soul, to fill me with your empathy and compassion.*
> *I ask you, my soul, to fill me with your insight and purpose.*
> *I ask you, my soul, to fill me with your wisdom, knowledge, and understanding.*
> *I ask you, my soul, to fill me with your thoughts and ideas.*
> *I ask you, my soul, to fill me with your words, phrases, and sentences.*
> *I ask you, my soul, to fill me with your voice so that it may spill out onto all those I speak to today and tonight.*

*I ask you, my soul, to fill me with your strength and courage.*

*I ask you, my soul, to fill me with your clarity and vision.*

*I ask you, my soul, to fill me with your hope, faith, and belief.*

*I ask you, my soul, to fill me with your optimism and positivity.*

*I ask you, my soul, to fill me with your confidence and power.*

*I ask you, my soul, to fill me with your love and have your love exude from my pores and spill out onto all those I encounter today and tonight.*

*I ask you, my soul, to fill me with your grace.*

*I ask you, my soul, to fill me with your patience and tolerance.*

*I ask you, my soul, to fill me with your creativity, expansion, and growth.*

*I ask you, my soul, to fill me with your curiosity and inquisitive nature.*

*I ask you, my soul, to guide me today and tonight in all things I do.*

*I ask you, my soul, to take away my anger.*

*I ask you, my soul, to take away my resentment.*

*I ask you, my soul, to take away my fear.*

*I ask you, my soul, to take away my anxiety.*

*I ask you, my soul, to take away my insecurity.*

*I ask you, my soul, to take away my doubt.*

*I ask you, my soul, to take away my shame.*

*I ask you, my soul, to take away my confusion.*
*I ask you, my soul, to take away my procrastination.*
*I ask you, my soul, to take away my self-centered ego.*
*I ask you my soul, to take away my negativity.*
*I ask you, my soul, to take away all my addictions.*

## Dialogue

*Now that you are connected to your soul, it is time to take out your journal. You will be dialoguing with your soul, so be certain that you are clear with the questions you ask. Write a question in your journal and then say out loud, "I ask you, my soul, to answer my question."*

*Put your pen on the paper, and your soul will respond to you.*

*Here are a few questions you may want to ask, but the rest is up to you.*

1. *What is the most important thing that you want me to know?*
2. *What can I do to take better care of myself?*
3. *How can I learn to fully forgive myself?*
4. *Is there something that I am unaware of that is hurting me?*
5. *What direction should I proceed in with my life?*
6. *How can I learn to love myself completely?*
7. *What is the most important thing for me to focus on right now?*

When you become soul-oriented, your whole life will begin to change. Those guilty feelings that you have been holding on to will leave your consciousness. The anger that is just below the surface will release itself. Your confidence and self-esteem will soar, and you will feel connected to a higher purpose. This is the real you. This is the you that wants to emerge and participate in a new story. This is the you that will never have to struggle with addictive cycles ever again.

# 5 | FRUSTRATION, ANNOYANCE, AND RESENTMENT

When I was a boy, I had a terrible temper. I was known for it. It seemed like the smallest things would set me off. I was a perfectionist, and whenever I performed less than my (perceived) capability, my frustration would boil over. I would throw my baseball bat against the chain-link fence if I didn't get a hit. If I got anything below an A on my report card, I would rip it up, throw it in the trash, and cry. I blazed through my early days smashing things and feeling like a failure. My parents would constantly bark at me, "Carder, you have got to learn to control your temper." But I had no idea how. And when they called me out, I only felt worse. I was embarrassed and ashamed by my behavior, but no one ever showed me a way to rectify it. At nine years old, I did not realize that frustration is linked to having expectations and needing control. So why am I talking about my bad temper in childhood? I believe that anger is addictive. The three types of anger I'll discuss here—frustration, annoyance, and resentment—each have addictive energies, but those energies can be disrupted if we know how.

We all feel angry sometimes. It is part of the human condition. Everyone handles it differently. Some yell; some mutter expletives; others slam doors, throw things, drive like maniacs on the freeway, punch each other; some cry. Depending on who sees us act out, we often regret it. When we are caught in a fury, we are usually not at our best. Our suffering is transmittable, or so we think, and we become a wrecking ball, leaving a swath of destruction in our wake. Some of us do the opposite: we keep our anger inside. We say nothing, shut down, and pretend like everything is okay. But swallowing our anger is also not okay.

When we hold on to our anger and bury it deep in our psyche, we create psychological illness in the body and mind. Anger turned inward transforms into shame, depression, anxiety, grief, and physical disease. Our bodies and minds are interconnected in a delicate way and affect one another on a daily basis. If you are angry with someone, you may feel the muscles in your neck tighten or your stomach turn. There is no denying that the repression of negative emotion has physical conse-quences. Those who keep their anger inside may feel that acting out is a bad thing—that it demonstrates immaturity or lack of control—so they hide it as best they can. But one way or another, it always comes out.

There are temperaments that don't tend to feel angry easily, but for the rest of us, we need to learn healthy ways to manage our frustrations. Have you ever watched someone de-escalate their own frustration by taking a few deep breaths, walking away from an argument, or calming themselves with a few reassuring words? It is a marvel to see and a model for all of us to follow. But frustration is a funny thing. The very nature of it impedes our ability to make good choices in the moment. When we are triggered, it is as if we are possessed—and in a way, we are, in that our bodies are flooded by stress hormones.

As a kid, I had an urge deep inside to let this negative energy out. That, in essence, was what drove me to tell a teacher to "Go fuck yourself" in sixth grade. The compulsion was too strong, and I had no strategy to diffuse it, so even though I knew it was wrong, I said it. This is one of the truest markers of addictive behavior—knowing that our actions will lead to unpleasant repercussions but not being able to control our behavior.

Annoyance is a bitter form of anger that rides just below the surface. It is mainly present when we are disturbed by something that sours our mood, but we remain on a low simmer (where full-on anger is beyond the boiling point). Perhaps the mailman continues to put your mail in the neighbor's mailbox, even when you politely ask him not to do so. Really annoying. Or a friend tells you they will meet you at 7:00 p.m.

but doesn't show up until 7:30 p.m., and you have lost your dinner reservation. Beyond annoying. Annoyance frequently takes up residence in the family household—it is not uncommon for spouses (*Why do they always put the forks in the drawer upside down!*) or siblings (*Why does the music have to be so loud?*) to feel annoyed with each other. We look at situations from our perspective and cannot understand why someone is unwilling to fulfill our needs or comply with our preferences. In this way, annoyance is ego-based; it's part of expressing our independence, our point of view. Feeling it sometimes is normal. But why do some of us feel annoyed so often?.

If it's persistent, it can mean that some aspect of our own lives is disturbing us. Because we are dissatisfied with a part of ourselves, we project that part onto someone else. We fixate on their supposed offense as the source of our discontent, not realizing that what really ails us lies deeper. It's much easier to shrug off misaligned forks when nothing else is bothering you.

There is an obsessive element to annoyance that fits under our definition of addictive thoughts. When we are annoyed, most of our other thoughts are overtaken by the energy of anger, and we become single-mindedly focused on our grievance. It is difficult to focus on anything else when we are annoyed, and until we engage in some sort of offensive, the distraction continues. It is the fly that keeps buzzing around our head. As with frustration, we have different ways of reacting. Some of us do nothing about the fly, but our irritation grows with every buzz until we explode. Others immediately drop everything and chase it around the room, shouting obscenities. Neither is ideal. Remaining calm and patient, with the flyswatter at hand, always works better than swinging wildly.

Another common form of anger is the uneasy feeling of resentment. Resentment is more passive than frustration and annoyance, as it usually remains dormant for quite some time. It is the sense that we have been slighted in some way by a person or an institution— that we have been ignored or disrespected, passed over or taken for granted. Resentments are extremely toxic and build over time. Unlike frustration or annoyance, resentment does not hold an immediate charge. Instead, while frustration and annoyance fade, resentment lasts and lasts. When we feel mistreated by others, the seeds of resentment are planted. As further resentments collect around it, they flourish, taking up more and more space in the psyche. If we allow them to grow, there is the danger of psychological and physical illness. We treat resentments as if they are guarded secrets, unable to reveal them even to ourselves. In many cases, we are unaware that they exist, only knowing that we feel heavily laden with unrest and negativity. Resentments can upend our peaceful existence by diverting us from the path of the soul.

The true test of resentment is simple: at a time when you're feeling emotionally calm, think about a specific person. What is the first emotion that arises? If you remain calm or perhaps smile, then this person holds no power over you. If you instantly feel uncomfortable, distressed, or unsettled, there is something more there, and resentment could very well be present. Resentments thrive in a victim mentality. They take root in the ego, as we feel our sense of self is under attack. And even if we are aware that they are there, most of us have no idea how to uproot them.

Much of the time, our resentments are decades old and have been wreaking havoc on our psychological immune system the whole time. The most common case of resentment I have treated in my private practice is a prolonged dissatisfaction with our parents. And these feelings of deep anger do not magically resolve themselves when a parent dies; quite the contrary, they gain strength. Upon their death, we realize that there will be no resolution, and this may contribute to feelings of guilt or hopelessness. In my case, the resentment I had toward my father became rocket fuel for the suffering and disillusionment that accompanied my substance abuse. I was addicted to the feeling of anger, and my compulsive act was to self-medicate. It seemed that the only way to soothe my constant ire toward him was to continuously hurt myself. Not very logical, but neither is addiction.

My father was a heroic figure in my life until I was twelve years old. At that time I learned that he had been cheating on my mother with numerous women in clandestine affairs. My mother was so distraught that she filed for divorce and proceeded to drown herself in a bottle of vodka. My mother died from alcoholism in 2012—she never put the bottle down after the divorce.

Although it read "acute ethanol poisoning" on her death certificate, I believe that she died from a broken heart. When my parents split up, my older brother, who was my best friend, went to live with my father, and I stayed with my mother. That was my parents' legal agreement, and I hated my father for this. Not only had he shattered my mother's heart, but he robbed me of my dear brother. I blamed him for destroying my childhood, and the resentment led to serious psychological illness. I suffered from eating disorders for the decade that followed and then turned to alcohol and substances until the age of thirty-five.

The trauma of my parents' divorce and the agony that followed had a stranglehold on my psyche that I could not shake. Nothing was the same after that, and I fell into a depression that followed me through my teen years. Although the event had passed, it continued to affect me until I finally faced it in therapy. This is what resentment does—it holds us captive.

So, how does this fit into our picture of addiction? Resentments are often comprised of an interpretation of events in the past, and when we fall prey to them, it is difficult to be present. There is a nagging feeling of discontent; we obsess about it relentlessly. They can be strong enough to distract our focus and consume our mental energy. When we think about that person or situation, we sit in judgment and blame, caught in a loop of obsessive cognition. If we try to repress the thoughts, they land in the body and create disease and sickness. These thoughts lead to all kinds of compulsive behaviors, such as self-medication (as I did), displacement of aggression, or even isolation. Whatever the behavior, it is most often a maladaptive coping strategy. In other words, it may work for a moment, but the resentment always returns. Some people will carry resentments to their deathbed and in those final moments of life will still be burdened by unresolved anger. This doesn't have to happen. You have the power to uproot your resentments. I will show you how.

Each one of us has core values that we intend to live by. When we feel confident, unburdened by guilt, and joyful, we are in alignment with our values. And when we actively (or passively) stand against one of our values, we feel it. Sometimes it is subtle—a shift in mood, a burst of anxiety, a judgmental thought—but we feel it nonetheless. We are not actually angry at the situation that confronts us but angrier with ourselves for doing something we know is wrong. This is hard for most to admit, so we continue to cite the infractions of others as the reason. Even if we are unable to pinpoint an external cause of our internal strife, we recognize that somewhere deep within us, we are discontented.

Let's look at honesty for a moment. It is fair to say that most people claim honesty as a core value. But how many of you are really honest? I mean honest to a fault? There are so many possible deviations from rigorously honest behavior that many of us believe we're honest when we are not. If someone asks you how you are doing and you reply, "Very well, thank you," but in actuality you're having an abysmal day, this is not an honest answer. If you are trying to impress someone and act in a way that is out of character, this is not honest behavior. Even if you are stretching the truth to benefit someone else or to avoid conflict, you are still being untruthful. We may excuse our dishonesty as a normal part of complicated human dynamics, but this does not alter the fact that it is hurtful—mainly to ourselves.

And being honest *with ourselves* is another story. We often justify or minimize our falsehoods in order to consciously protect our ego, but underneath we are creating a rupture in our own psyche. If honesty is one of your core values and you are not being completely honest, then there will likely be consequences. Each time we act in a way that is misaligned with our moral compass, we emotionally traumatize ourselves. We are the ones who suffer as the emotional trauma solidifies into anger in its various forms. We are quicker to frustration, quicker to annoyance. So, how do we deal with this anger? It is through compassion that we will find our way again.

Compassion is a core value that many of us share. It is a deep understanding and acceptance of the conditions of others. This acceptance comes with an attitude of nonjudgment and an attempt to sympathize with and ease the suffering of others. When we are compassionate, we look at others with loving eyes and blanket them with forgiveness, no matter what they have done. This is not always easy and requires an outlook of patience and tolerance. Compassion exists in all of us— it is embedded in the true nature of all human beings. It is archetypal and familiar in a way that most of our core values are. This is because our core values are the voice of the soul. We are born with them in our DNA, and they are reinforced by the lessons we learn throughout life.[18] When we are in complete alignment with our core values, we are allowing our soul to govern us, not our ego.

I finally forgave my father when I was about thirty-six years old. It felt like someone had lifted a thousand pounds off my chest. I had always seen him as the perpetrator of my misfortunes. I believed that his thoughtless actions were responsible for my unhappiness and addiction. Every time I got high, I justified my self-destruction by pointing to him as the cause. But I was wrong—dead wrong. It was not the things he did that kept me high, but the resentment I held inside. The resentment I had allowed to thrive, spurning my strongly held core value of compassion. When I dedicated myself to hearing his story, I became deeply moved. He had a difficult upbringing in a military family and had gone to eleven different schools in his first ten years of life. He did not meet his father until he was seven years old, as my grandfather was fighting in World War II until then. I cannot imagine how that must have felt. Ultimately, I realized that my father was full of flaws and imperfections, just like me. He was full of contradictions, hubris,

18  Gareth Cook, "The Moral Life of Babies," *Scientific American* (Springer Nature America Inc., November 12, 2013), https://www.scientificamerican.com/article/the-moral-life-of-babies/.

anger, and vanity, but underneath was always that small boy who felt abandoned.

In truth, my father suffered his whole life. This is what I came to understand, and it totally altered my perspective. What I have discovered as a psychologist is that this is an archetypal story that most of us share. We go through tremendous pain and heartache as human beings and try the best we can to cope, but most of us fall short. Unfortunately, my father did not have the benefit of spirituality to heal him. The only "soul" he came to know was the leather one on the bottom of his lace-up shoe. He died as a man full of regret. I have tremendous compassion for my father, and this element of the soul has saved my life.

It was compassion that finally taught me how to forgive. By recognizing that the flaws of others were the same misgivings I had in myself, I began to see myself differently. I had been holding on to a lot of shame and guilt about my drug addiction and all the deceptive behavior that it caused. The judgment that had always festered in me started to dissipate, and I slowly became humble. I forgave my father for his struggles—and I forgave myself. I realized that compassion was not just something to offer others but something to offer myself. Self-compassion became a cornerstone of my ethical conduct. I engage in the process of forgiving myself on a regular basis, and as a result, my anger has dissipated. The more I am aligned with the core values that are created by my soul, the happier I become. This is now a daily practice for me. I urge you to try it for yourself.

**Exercise**

**Aligning with Your Core Values**

*Take out a piece of paper and write down your core values. I suggest starting with five, although you may have more. These are five of the principles that you hold in the highest esteem and aspire to live by. Next to each of your core values, write a few sentences determining whether or not you are in alignment with it. Use this sheet as a guide every day. Remember that your core values come from your soul, and when you are aligned with them, you are in accordance with the will of your soul.*

*Below is an example.*

**Honesty:** *I stretched the truth today when I spoke to my sister about my opinion of her situation. I wasn't honest with myself when I minimized the importance of limiting my sugar intake.*

**Integrity:** *I was a bit lazy today and procrastinated when I should have been writing.*

**Kindness:** *In alignment.*

**Compassion:** *I was judgmental of the guy who ticketed my car.*

**Patience:** *I was short and intolerant with my kids when they were arguing.*

If you are out of alignment with some of your core values, there is a good possibility you will feel frustrated and irritable. When confronted by a similar situation in the days that follow, make an attempt to modify your thought or behavior. Don't get discouraged if you fall short—forgive yourself and move on, treating each day as a new opportunity. As time goes by, you'll learn more about yourself and find it easier to discern and act in accordance with your core values. The addictive energy of anger and the compulsion to express it will be significantly dampened. When you live within the confines of your system of morality, your whole outlook on life will feel different. Your self-esteem will grow, and your fear will subside. When we are aligned with the soul, there are no negative emotions that impede our growth. When the soul is present, there is no room for addiction to thrive. Give it a try.

# 6 | ALCOHOL AND DRUGS

**D**espite being simply distilled grains, boiled potatoes, and fermented fruits and vegetables in liquid form, alcohol has captured the global imagination for thousands of years. Alcohol has unique properties that connoisseurs around the world love. Spirits that are aged in a barrel for one hundred years, wines that deliver a woodsy aromatic bouquet, amber beers from a neighborhood microbrewery that are the talk of the town—people love their brand, their flavor, their type.

But it is what alcohol does to the mind that captivates most of us, as we seek it out to make us feel different. Many people use it as a release to bulldoze their inhibitions and celebrate their accomplishments. Drinking can be a way to connect with others, reveal our true feelings, and enhance a Saturday afternoon with revelry and laughter. There is no harm in any of these pursuits—quite the contrary. Psychologically, it is healthy to let your hair down from time to time and not take yourself so seriously. The occasional use of alcohol, if handled with precaution, can be a good way to let loose or relax and unwind.

It's safe to assume that we have all seen someone drunk. On television, at a wedding, out to dinner, or at a happy hour. The classic signs are well-known: stumbling around, slurring words, maybe crying uncontrollably, picking fights, or otherwise acting completely out of character. Well, that's what alcohol does to people when it is consumed in quantity. Some people just need a few sips and they are off to the races, while others have built up a significant tolerance and barely show signs of inebriation even when they drink a lot. When someone overdoes it, they pay the price. They do something they regret and feel ashamed the next day, or they wake up with a hangover the size of Detroit. Some people swear off alcohol for a while. But when caught in an addictive cycle, this logical application of self-preservation does not apply. If the energy of addiction is present, there will be no stopping.

If it is not the alcohol that poses the problem or threat, then what does? I have heard it argued multiple times in the rooms of Alcoholics Anonymous that the person, not the alcohol, is the culprit—that alcoholics are not built like other people.[19] This AA theory is based on the premise that alcoholics have tendencies that others do not, for example, self-centeredness, dishonesty, and a controlling nature. I find this premise to be shortsighted and suspiciously too pat. I have found that most people have these qualities to some degree, and they have nothing to do with their alcohol consumption. AA also states that alcoholism is a disease.[20] I would argue that when someone is in the midst of an addictive cycle fueled by obsessive thoughts and compulsive actions, they're certainly in a state of dis-ease. But there is no disease of the mind here, just a buildup of harmful energy that powers repetitive behaviors.

Addictive thinking is propelled by the idea that the alcohol is soothing medicine that alleviates our emotional pain. The fact is that life on earth is no cakewalk. Most people experience some kind of suffering every day, whether it is physical pain, emotional discomfort, insecurity, fear, doubt, or dissatisfaction. Yes, the suffering of humanity is palpable—just turn on the news and you will see examples of it. But people don't usually drink because they witness someone else's pain; it is their own pain that drives them to drink. This

19  Gabrielle Glaser, "The Irrationality of Alcoholics Anonymous," *The Atlantic*, April 2015, https://www.theatlantic.com/magazine/archive/2015/04/the-irrationality-of-alcoholics-anonymous/386255/.

20  "This Is A.A.: An Introduction to the A.A. Recovery Program" (New York: Alcoholics Anonymous World Services Inc., 2017), 9–11.

emotional strife is archetypal and can be found in the earliest myths and folklore we have on record. Human beings have always suffered immensely.

Trauma is a concept that is often misconstrued and thought of in a physical context. We may consider trauma to be the result of a catastrophic event—an earthquake, a hurricane, the lived experience of war, sexual abuse. While these certainly fit into the category of trauma, there are many forms that are more subtle and universal. Emotional trauma is a prevalent force behind the addictive cycles that fuel the compulsive consumption of alcohol. People often dismiss this type of trauma, but I assure you it is real. It may be the product of our childhoods and the negative experiences we internalized growing up. A baby who is neglect-fully left in the crib without constant attention and love will feel trauma. A child who has narcissistic parents, or parents who are consumed by their own confusion and suffering, will feel trauma. An adolescent who is bullied, left out, teased, and shamed for being different will experience trauma. Any moment in our lives that we feel dismissed, abandoned, rejected, or judged unfairly, we are encountering a traumatic situation. Unlike other emotions that come and go, trauma stays. We do not have the capacity to release it, and this makes us vulnerable. With all this trauma floating around in the psyche, we may feel displaced, uneasy, and even depressed. We carry a heavy load of negative emotion, and the effects are devastating.

Negative thoughts about ourselves are a trauma

response that may ultimately constellate into limiting beliefs, which create a false narrative about our value. We create a story about who we are according to the complicated moments of our lives. This is an archetypal pattern that you will find with most everyone who is caught in an addictive cycle. We all have these beliefs, even though we may not be aware of them. The most common beliefs that I hear from my patients are deeply rooted in their own history. I hear them say, "I don't feel like I'm good enough" or "I'm never going to be happy—that's just the way it is" or "I'm not smart." (All untrue, by the way.) Limiting beliefs create gaps in our psychological immune system that may allow the energy of addiction to penetrate our core.

Recently, I treated a thirty-five-year-old woman who was struggling with mixed anxiety and addiction. She had a good job, made plenty of money, was in a loving relationship with her husband, and had a gaggle of close friends. On the outside it would appear that her life was enviable, wonderful even, but on the inside her beliefs were standing in the way of her happiness. Although she had amassed a number of the things that would tradi-tionally lead to fulfillment, she was constantly burdened by a feeling of inferiority—that her life would never amount to anything. When she received validation from her husband or colleagues at work, she never really believed them. Their words could not penetrate the fortress of low self-esteem that had been erected around her soul.

She also mistrusted the motives of others and felt

like the rug could be pulled from under her feet at any moment. She actually expected it to be, and the fear became overwhelming. But no one knew about any of this, as she was afraid to reveal her true feelings, even to her husband. She felt that he might leave her if she showed her vulnerability.

She began drinking every night. She started with wine at dinner, but over time a glass had turned into a bottle. At first, she believed that it lightened her mood, but she began to have panic attacks in the morning. The wine remained, and she soon added bourbon before dinner and hid a flask in her desk that she nipped at every hour. Whenever she was overcome by fear, she felt that the bottle was her only ally. The alcohol soothed her in the moment, but the negative feelings came back—they always do. She wasn't honest with her husband and told no one except me about her drinking. I advised her that she alone had the ability to heal herself, and that when she did, the addictive cycle would vanish. And it did.

We had to dig for a while to find out what her negative and limiting beliefs were, but when we found them, it all made sense. She had grown up in a middle-class family. Her father worked long hours and was rarely at home. Her mother was clinically depressed but never diagnosed and took no medication for her ailment. From a very early age, my patient took care of her mother. After school, she would try to wake her mother from a perpetual afternoon nap; she would comb her hair and make her food. She wanted nothing more than to make her mother feel better, but her mother rarely cracked a smile.

It was clear that she had experienced significant emotional trauma as a child and even into her adulthood. She spoke of never feeling safe. She relayed an incident when she was seven years old—one of the first memories she could recall. She woke up on a Saturday morning. She knew that her father was at work, and when she went downstairs, there was no sign of her mother. She called out to her mother, searched every room in the house, but she was nowhere. She was frightened and had no idea what to do. She didn't know how to use the telephone to call her father and did not know the neighbors well enough to ask for help. She sat on the kitchen floor, terrified, for an hour until her mother returned from the grocery store. Her mother belittled the incident and said that it was no big deal—that she was a big girl and old enough to take care of herself. From this point forward, she was afraid of being left alone. She told me she felt like her parents did not care about her.

We identified two limiting beliefs that began at age seven. One was that she felt unwanted and so never believed she was good enough. The other was that she never felt safe. Not feeling valuable or trusting of others are two common beliefs that many of my patients share—regardless of the type of emotional trauma they endured in childhood. It is remarkable how many adults feel this way. But the prevalence of these beliefs does not make them true.

Remember, these are human beliefs created by the ego—they are not the natural beliefs that emanate from the soul. The soul's beliefs are untainted by the harsh realities of living in the world. The soul's beliefs are firmly anchored in our psyche, but emotional trauma buries them under a powerful false narrative. The soul will express that you are kind, valuable, worthy, and beautiful—but you cannot hear its voice when the trauma within you remains unexcavated. The voice you hear instead—the one that repeats your limiting beliefs like dark mantras—is nearly impossible to silence without the soul's intervention. I will teach you how to stop these voices and change the distorted opinion you have about yourself. Your soul is asking you to do this.

I asked my patient if she had any photographs of herself when she was seven years old. I told her to carry them around with her for a few days and put them in prominent places in her home so she could view them regularly. When she felt very familiar with the images of her younger self, I offered her an exercise. It is called the Time Angel, and it is a practice that I teach most of my patients. The premise is that the psyche does not differentiate the events we experience in real life from the ones we imagine. They have equal validity and potency in the unconscious, and therefore what we imagine has the ability to heal our wounds. I'll give you an example: if you were on a hike yesterday and watched a beautiful red and orange sunset bounce off the clouds, and the sunset made you feel serene, that feeling is still available to you today. Just close your eyes and imagine the same sunset in all its glory. The serenity will wash over you again. This exercise refers directly to the soul, as the soul's language is based in images, thoughts, and feelings.

In the Time Angel, we revisit our younger self and act in the role of a loving parent to shift the narrative from negative thoughts to more accurate and constructive ones. We will replace the ego's limiting beliefs with ones from our soul. Once we have done this, our relationship to ourselves will change dramatically, and the way we see the world will transform.

## Exercise
### The Time Angel

### Part One

*Think about the negative beliefs you have about yourself. (We all have them, so don't be discouraged.) Do you feel inferior, unlovable, unsafe, not smart, victimized, not good enough, ugly, or weak? Do you feel as though you will never succeed in life? Do you feel insignificant or unworthy? Is there a voice telling you that you are a fraud and an impostor? These are a few of the common false, negative, and limiting beliefs that we collect over a lifetime. Try to pinpoint a few that apply to you. Write them down on a piece of paper.*

*Think about your childhood and the relationships you had with your parents, siblings, friends, and peers. Were there times that you felt abandoned, neglected, bullied, abused, or voiceless? We all share these moments. Our beliefs derive from these early experiences and relationships, so try to remember which ones were difficult. Try to match up an event that happened at a certain age with one of your negative beliefs. If your belief is that you are not smart, think of how and when it was implanted in your psyche. Was it a statement from a teacher, teasing on the playground, the lack of affirmation from your parents—or a combination of all these things? When you have identified the age and the incident or person that created this belief, write it down on the piece of paper as well.*

**Part Two**
*When you have identified how old you were when the limiting belief began, find a photo of yourself at that age and spend a few days looking it. When you have the image etched in your memory, find a quiet place in your home, turn off your phone, and shut down your computer and any other distractions. Close your eyes and imagine yourself sitting on a park bench on a beautiful sunny day in the summer. You see your younger self walking down the paved path toward you, and you smile as they sit down next to you. You introduce yourself as an older version of your younger self and say that you are there to clarify a few things.*

*Whatever the belief is that the younger self still clings to, let them know that it is not true. Let them know the reasons why it is a false belief. Explain well. Express to your younger self how bold, courageous, smart, strong, and cool they are and how proud you are of them. This is your opportunity to reparent your younger self, and they desperately need it. Let them know that from now on, you will always be with them and that you will visit with them every day.*

Do this ten-minute exercise every day for a month. Each time, address the different false beliefs that have accumulated. If you are aware that some of the beliefs began at other ages, visit those ages as well. Replace the ego-based negative beliefs with soul-based loving ones. Replace *I am not enough* with *I am strong and brave and a survivor.* The energy of addiction will not be present once these beliefs are altered. The compulsion to drink alcohol will leave you. You will look, feel, think, and act differently once you begin to live in the narrative that your soul has created for you.

## Substances

Chemical substances are similar to alcohol in their conquest of the fragile human psyche. There is an opioid crisis raging through the United States right now,[21] and no matter how many resources we throw at it, little appears to change. With opioids (heroin, oxycodone, Demerol) and benzodiazepines (Valium, Klonopin, lorazepam), there is a physical dependency in the body that mirrors the psychological obsession to take the drug. This dependency serves as a major

---

21 "Drug Overdose Deaths in the U.S. Top 100,000 Annually." Centers for Disease Control and Prevention, November 17, 2021. National Center for Health Statistics. https://www.cdc.gov/nchs/pressroom/nchs_press_releases/2021/20211117.htm.

deterrent toward sobriety, as detoxing from these substances is terribly difficult. The physical pain from withdrawal often overwhelms the desire to stop using. Sustained use of alcohol and nicotine also build up a dependency in the body.

The traditional way to treat these chemical dependencies in the US is with a thirty-day stay at an inpatient rehabilitation center, considered by many to be the most effective treatment option. I can tell you from firsthand knowledge that it's not. Unfortunately, inpatient treatment methods have increasingly fallen short in the past few decades. Greg Hannley, nationally recognized addiction expert and founder/CEO of multiple Soba Recovery Centers throughout the United States, once told me that the rate of continuous sobriety in the first year posttreatment is less than 10 percent.[22] These results are staggeringly low, the methods used are relatively ineffective, and the philosophy taught is outdated. But you will still see the TV ads blaring the promise of a better life from multiple seaside facilities up and down the coast. I worked as a therapist in multiple treatment centers for nearly a decade and can honestly tell you that they are making false assertions. I have worked with dozens of their patients who relapsed within two weeks of their release date.

Other folks flock to the meetings of Alcoholics and Narcotics Anonymous in an attempt to break

---

22  "Aftercare Planning Programs and Recovery: Soba Recovery," Soba Recovery Centers, December 30, 2020, https://sobarecovery.com/treatment/aftercare/.

their addictive cycles. While there are some benefits to these programs, they also fall short, in my opinion. I attended these meetings for a few years after I got sober and learned some principles that have helped me in my recovery, but it was the people in the room who made a difference. I forged friendships with other identified addicts and in doing so felt connected and not alone. This is the greatest benefit of the twelve-step program, in my view: the ability to meet others who have been through similar circumstances.

There is a little-known tree that grows in a small country named Gabon in central Africa. This remarkable shrub is called *Tabernanthe iboga*. Iboga is a sacred plant in the Bwiti spiritual tradition practiced by tribes indigenous to Gabon. Bwitists believe iboga was the first plant ever to be touched by divine consciousness, therefore holding sacred energy and wisdom in its roots. Bwitists have been actively taking these roots for thousands of years with incredible benefits both physically and emotionally.[23]

What the iboga roots contain is called ibogaine, a psychoactive alkaloid that, in large doses, induces a profound psychedelic state. One of the most unique characteristics of the iboga roots is that they eliminate the obsessive thinking and compulsive action that drive addiction. In an immediate and visceral way, iboga opens a pathway to the soul. Many of those who take it

---

23 Guide to Ibogaine - Experience, Benefits & Side Effects." Third Wave, April 19, 2022. https://thethirdwave.co/psychedelics/ibogaine/.

speak of a deliberate communion with their soul that is both real and humbling. Also, much like the exercise I provided you in this chapter, iboga expels all your false and limiting beliefs and replaces them with the voice of the soul. This was my experience when I took the plant medicine in the rain forest of Brazil.

I had been sober for a number of years when I had this experience, so it wasn't quitting drugs or alcohol that attracted me to the ritual. I was looking for clarity and hoping to gain insight on the nature of my path as I continued my work as a psychologist. I had no idea what to expect, really. The results were beyond my wildest imagination. It was a psychoactive and visual experience that allowed me to visit the depths of my psyche. I witnessed the process of my old thoughts being swept away. I was aware that I was in the presence of a consciousness far greater than my own—perhaps a divine one. I emerged from the ceremony feeling as though I was connected to my best self for the first time in my life. The plant medicine had scoured the crevasses in my unconscious and purged them of any doubt and negativity. I was whole again.

Although iboga is not legal in the United States, there are many countries, including Canada, Mexico, and Brazil, in which the plant is sanctioned by the government.[24] There are treatment facilities springing

---

24 Mandy Oaklander, "Inside Ibogaine, One of the Most Promising and Perilous Psychedelics for Addiction," *TIME,* April 12, 2021, https://time.com/5951772/ibogaine-drug-treatment-addiction/.

up across the globe that offer ibogaine to their patients with astounding efficacy toward curing addiction. Ibogaine is an extract of one of the most concentrated alkaloids of iboga and is used primarily to treat addiction. During a research visit to São Paulo, Brazil, I met with Dr. Bruno Ramos Gomez, a psychologist who works at the Ourinhos Hospital, which is now administering clinical trials with ibogaine. According to Dr. Gomez, the one-year sobriety rate of patients treated with ibogaine is somewhere around 70 percent, which is seven times greater than that of traditional treatment in the US, as previously mentioned in this chapter. The ibogaine treatment takes one day, and recipients walk away with relatively no cravings or withdrawal symptoms at all. The plant medicine has connected to their souls and has removed them.

It is unfortunate that scientists and doctors in America are so constrained by the regulations of a fearful government that has unsuccessfully attempted to treat addiction with pharmaceutical interventions for years. Most rehabs will try to detox you with chemicals such as methadone or Subutex and medicate you with a number of antidepressants and mood stabilizers. This simply creates other dependencies and, instead of solving the problem, makes it worse. That being said, in my professional opinion, the energy of addiction is best managed by spiritual means—that is, through a willingness to embrace your soul.

# 7 | NOT SO SMARTPHONES

**A** majority of us have them, the sleek minicomputers that fit in our hands. When we leave the house and perform a mental checklist of things we cannot forget—keys, sunglasses, wallet—our phone is on there. We believe that we can't function without it—that we'll be cut off from our ability to work, socialize, and check our email. In many cases, phones replaced meeting in person, even before the global pandemic that kept us from doing so. (The pandemic greatly increased our dependence on virtual communication, strengthening our compulsion to engage with our phones.) We simply press a button and video chat with our colleagues, friends, and family. For many of us, a video screen has interfered with experiencing the tangible aspects of human life. We hide behind it like a protective shield and disengage from the customs we know so well, like meeting in person or stopping by for a visit. And when we do sit down face-to-face, we get up from the table in the midst of a conversation to answer a text or receive a call—the natural flow of conversation constantly interrupted. There are consequences to these small moments that have changed the texture of human interaction on Planet Earth. We now behave differently because of our phones.

It wasn't always like this. I was twenty-six years old when I bought my first smartphone. It was a big, clunky one that didn't even have a text function. I remember thinking how great it was to have a mobile device that would allow me to be in contact with everyone I knew. I was so used to coming home and checking my answering machine for updates from my entourage regarding dinner plans and rendezvous. I looked forward to that—listening to everyone's voice in a single session and scrawling down messages in a notebook I kept by the house phone. I would call them back when I got a chance and relished in the freedom of space and time. No one knew when I walked in the door or where I was, and this provided me the luxury of autonomy—an ability to disengage that has vanished in recent years. I felt like I could breathe after a long day without immediate obligations. I could spend the first hour or two at home attending to myself. I miss those hours of freedom and often long for that era—one marked by a feeling of disembarkation from noise and people. An era of nonattachment to electronic devices.

What I remember most about my teenage years were the experiences I shared with my friends. There were road trips, weekend getaways, game nights at the pool table, beach bonfires, and romantic walks down lovers' lane. When I was in the company of others, there was an energy in the air that bound us together. It was the sanctity of unobstructed presence. There were no technological distractions to drive a wedge between us and no angst or alertness that our parents could disrupt the moment with a worried text message. We were on our own, for the most part, and this allowed us to really get to know one another. We became obsessed with each other's idiosyncrasies, ideas, and humor. We were in deep and listened intently to the stories we told and the words we spoke. These were magical times filled with exploration, mischief, rites of passage, and appreciation of one another. The bonds were forged by a mutual respect that grew out of our willingness to pay attention. There was an electricity to sharing the milestones that defined our young lives. We were present with each other, completely present, and this made all the difference. Many of the deep friendships I formed during my teenage years are still going strong today. I attribute this in part to the fact that we grew up without smartphones.

A patient of mine celebrated his daughter's sweet-sixteen birthday dinner at a restaurant. There was a mixture of teenage boys and girls at the table, and at one point during the dinner, they were all on their phones—every one of them. The most alarming part about this was that they were all communicating with one another, not with people who were absent from the celebration. Instead of looking across the table and speaking in words, they were looking down at their laps and writing texts. When I heard about this, I was saddened but not surprised, for this was a trend I had witnessed as well, and it was not unique to teenagers.

I've seen adults nearly run over by cars as they saunter past red lights and into the street while glued to their handheld screens. I've watched people walk into trees, bump into each other, and even fall down stairs. When I walk into my crowded local coffee shop, there is little noise emanating from people, as most of them are in conversation with their electronic devices. Even the ones who are conversing in person will exit their dialogue frequently to check their phones. What they are looking for escapes me—I have found that the most gratifying type of communication is marked by looking someone in the eyes and paying close attention to their expression. This is how I was brought up and what I believe to be respectful. So, how have the dynamics of human interaction become so fractured? Well, we have to look at the very nature of human beings to answer this question.

At a very young age, many of us had a stuffed animal or blanket that we carried with us everywhere we went. We needed them to feel secure—hence the name *security blanket*. Smartphones have become the adult version of a security blanket. We hide behind them when we need affirmation that we are not alone. Instead of being present with their surroundings in public, most people, especially when they are alone, are focused on a small screen in their hands. Before smartphones, people would interact with one another in these settings, but the magnetic pull of these devices is just too strong. Not only do they allow us to immerse ourselves in a plethora of online activities, but they also protect our fragile self-esteem from the admission of unpopularity. We are no longer faced with the humiliation of public aloneness, for when we note others in our periphery, they are engrossed in their phones as well. Phones keep us separate, disconnected, and unaware of our surroundings—but they keep us safe.

Many of us are in a relationship with our phones. We treat our phones as if they were a close friend or even a romantic partner. They remain with us at all times, and we give them more attention than probably anything else. We rely on them for love and affection, much like they were living, breathing entities. They make us smile, flirt with us, and stroke our ego. We caress them as if they were someone's hand and sleep with them in our bed. This is a love affair gone wrong. One aspect of codependence is to derive our feelings about ourselves from external validation. We do this through people all the time, gauging our self-worth by the reactions and compliments of others. The phone has exploded these codependent tendencies as we seek perpetual endorsements on its many apps and platforms.

And what is the fallout from a romantic partnership with this small shiny object? Multiple psychological infirmities arise from it—the loop of obsessive thinking and compulsive action merely being one of them. We look each other in the eyes less. Phones have stunted our listening skills and ability to remain present in conversation. Most people do not put their phones away when they are with others, so they become a barrier to our ability to experience empathy—which requires attentiveness and focus. How many times have you been with someone whose phone keeps buzzing while you attempt to get a word in edgewise? Beyond the suffering communication skills, the artificial affirmation people receive from their phones may deter them from wanting to see others in person. If they are introverted or have social anxiety, the phone becomes a buffer, an excuse, a crutch. Smartphones have become a way to self-medicate—to soothe our negative emotions and fears, just like drugs and alcohol. But unlike the brief high of substances, phones do not always bring us momentary joy—quite the contrary.

Even as we seek affirmation via various apps and platforms, smartphones are the source of lingering anxiety for many of us. In some cases, self-esteem has become inextricably linked to the number of likes or views we receive on social media posts. We look at Instagram and marvel at the snapshots of other people's lives—they all look so darn happy. We compare, and our own lives suddenly seem less interesting, glamorous, or meaningful. Smartphones host such a broad variety of platforms—social media, texting, email, news outlets, the internet—that it is easy to lose ourselves. This lends itself to an obsessive type of thinking, as there are a multitude of ways to be drawn in: the allure of recognition when someone accepts or requests our online friendship, or an email that awaits a reply. Reaching out, be it via friend request, sent email, or text, creates uneasiness and anxiety more often than not. We obsess about the possibility that someone is deliberately ignoring us if our query remains unanswered. The longer we wait, the more we worry and feel compelled to check our phone. This is a clear picture of an addictive cycle taking shape. The obsession is these negative thoughts, and the compulsion is an incessant desire to check our phones. Even as we grow overwhelmed by the negativity, we can't stop looking.

But how have we become so enmeshed with our phones in the first place? This is a complicated question with the most straightforward answer being calculated manipulation. These devices are called smartphones for a reason—they are explicitly designed to appeal to our particular human sensibilities. Once you google something on your phone or make a purchase, your phone will then begin to offer you similar purchase ideas, images, and solicitations that fit your algorithm. If you search the web for tennis shoes, you will begin to see shoes and other apparel pop into your feed. One could argue that this provides a convenience for consumers, but in actuality your phone is now programmed to think for you. You are now a marketer's target. This is a dangerous game, and it renders many helpless— exploiting their tendencies to spend more money or time than they should. And not only products are hawked directly to you on various platforms—even the information you receive is at the whim of an algorithm. Google will show different results to different people. The age of misinformation has American culture devastatingly fractured, and the cause of our polarization is in the palm of our hands.

In recent years, social media platforms have also led to a troubling number of psychological issues, chiefly among children and teens. The term *Facebook depression* was coined by the American Academy of Pediatrics as a syndrome that plagues users with feelings of unworthiness, low self-esteem, and obscurity.[25] These feelings may arise when a user is being ignored, insulted, or cyberbullied. Cyberbullying includes sending hurtful, misleading, or shaming messages to someone—even posting them on a person's site for everyone to view. This virtual form of aggression has contributed to many teen suicides in the past decade. There are also the online predators that search for naive, unsuspecting victims to seduce or extort. Meeting online has become commonplace among romantic partners, but dating apps are ripe for misuse and have turned dating conventions upside down. Yes, your phone is dangerous and full of platforms and apps that open the door to a harmful ego-based narrative.

---

25 Gwenn Schurgin O'Keeffe, Kathleen Clarke-Pearson, Council on Communications and Media, "The Impact of Social Media on Children, Adolescents, and Families." *Pediatrics* April 2011; 127 (4): 800–804. https://doi.org/10.1542/peds.2011-0054.

For the last ten years, I have had a hard-and-fast rule in my therapy office—I ask that my patients power down their phones in the waiting room before they enter. Powering the phone down completely creates a different energy than switching to airplane mode, and I have noticed my patients relax in a different way when they are fully unplugged. My patients thank me for this edict—many of them tell me that this will be the only time during the week their phone is off. Some of them have no idea how to turn the phone on and off, as they have never done so before. About half of them are onboard or compliant, yet many a phone has beeped during a session after a patient has assured me it's off. The angst of being without their phone, even for a brief fifty-minute stint, is cause for them to be dishonest with their psychologist. In fact, a handful of people have left my practice expressly because of the phone guidelines. It has been an interesting, accidental experiment on human nature in the age of technology. I see how attached people are to their phones. They will lie, argue, justify, and demand that it be on and available at all times. Now, you tell me—do you think this is healthy? Does it feel familiar to you? Do you know how to turn your phone off?

When I get home from work, I practice another ritual. I check my phone to see if any urgent matter needs a response, and after completing this task, I shut it down—completely. Between the hours of 7:00 p.m. and 7:00 a.m., I am phone-free. This felt strange at first, as I too had built up a dependency on it, but after a while it began to seem normal. I was returning to the days of my childhood, before smartphones were invented. I cannot tell you how refreshing it feels to unplug from the constant give-and-take with my phone. I focus my energy on cultivating my relationships with my two children and my wife. We read stories together, talk about our days, work on puzzles, play games, and eat uninterrupted meals. I believe that this time is sacred—I will never get it back again, and it should be optimized. My kids will thank me for it someday, but in a way they already do, as their joy is linked to the amount of time I give them. They have not grown up in a household culture where phones are held in high esteem and therefore don't know differently. My relationships have improved since implementing these boundaries, and this comes as no surprise to me.

The soul promotes the expansion of human experience, not the contraction of it. From the soul's perspective, smartphones impede the primal, innate desire to commingle with one another, and they alter the way we perceive the people in our lives—even the ones we hold dearest. Remember, the soul is our biggest asset when it comes to healing. Its main purpose is to show us alternatives to our negative and ego-driven pursuits and help us to restore happiness and love in our psyche. The soul is ever-flowing, unshakable, and impervious to harm. It is the one constant in our lives that determines how we authentically feel and consistently pushes us to be better. The soul is much more interested in the cultivation of human relationships through direct experience rather than by artificial means. The phone is purely a product of ego, and addiction loves anything ego-driven. The soul cherishes freedom, while the ego is seduced by entanglement. The soul knows that one should not rely on validation or compliments to establish one's sense of self, but the ego derives its nature from this very exchange.

Daily changes can make a big difference. When you are not using it, you should put your smartphone away. When you are with others, switch to airplane mode and focus your attention completely on the person in front of you. It is hard to concentrate when an audible little beep alerts you to a new notification. Turn off notifications, or leave your phone on silent and enjoy the time you have with others.

## Exercises

*One day this week, your smartphone will be just a phone. There will be no text function or handheld computer available—silence those notifications if you can. You will simply use it to make telephone calls. When you are not using your phone, place it somewhere out of sight. Put it in your bag or on a shelf at home. If it rings, pick it up, but for any little beeps or dings, leave it alone. It may feel strange not to have it in your hand or pocket, but let it go. Your smartphone is not an extension of you. It is an entirely independent device.*

*This week, your phone is not your calendar, either. Print a weekly schedule page from your computer or go buy a daily planner. Begin to write down your appointments on the paper or in the book. Are you feeling retro yet? Actually, you may see this is a much better way to keep yourself organized. There is something about writing things down that helps to lodge them in the brain. This will help you be on time, prepared, and more present during your busy day. Anyone you normally text throughout the day, schedule a time to see or speak to that person. Yes, call them up and set a time to have coffee. Grab a bite after work or settle in for a real phone chat. Mark it down the old-fashioned way.*

*Pick a time every night when you will power your phone down. When you have turned it off, place it somewhere that it is not visible. Make an attempt to be unplugged from your phone for twelve hours at a time. Spend this time with the people you love or taking care of yourself. Read a (physical) book; exercise. The ability to be comfortable in one's own/your own company can be a positive thing, so long as it does not lead to prolonged self-isolation.*

*Before you go to bed at night, shut off your Wi-Fi, as long no one in your household is using it. Simply turn it off at the switch on the back of your router. There are also timers you can purchase that will do this for you. Wi-Fi is proven to emit a strong electromagnetic pulse that some believe has negative consequences. One of these is the disruption of healthy sleep. Do an experiment for a week and see if you sleep better. If you like the results, make this part of your nightly routine. I do this at night and have never slept better.*

*So many people spend hours perusing social media. This is a waste of precious time and not a healthy way to interact with others. At the most, make one post in the morning and check it again at night. Fifteen minutes each day is ample time to engage with other people's photos—especially if you curate your feed by following only accounts that don't bring up negative thoughts. If you see a post that you like, certainly comment, but make a mental note that you will reach out to that person sometime soon. Drop them a note or give them a call to catch up. The best-case scenario is once again to schedule a time to see them in person. If you use social media for your business, set a schedule on usage and stick to it. No matter why you use social media, be aware of mindless scrolling and close the app the moment you catch yourself doing it.*

*If you need to check your email, sit down at a computer to do so—do not use your phone. If you work at a computer, it is inevitable that you will constantly peruse your email. This is fine. But when you're not working, there is no need—make a habit of turning your computer off. Check your email once in the morning, again in the early afternoon, and once at night. Three email checks per day is more than enough.*

Try these changes for a week and begin to tell yourself that this is the new way. You may feel some anxiety, but push through it. Imagine the time that you will have to spend with your loved ones or out in nature. You will begin to be present with your surroundings and the people that you cherish. They will thank you for this. Less time on your devices means more time for what makes life well-lived.

# 8 | SEX, LOVE, AND PORN

Let's assume that all of us have been in love at some point. When it is pure, it feels incredible; there is nothing quite like it. We are born with love in our being—our brand-new cells are saturated with it, and in our first breath, we exhale it into the world. In fact, when we are infants, our wholehearted essence is driven by giving and receiving love, without thought or hesitation. We are little love machines churning with a desire for warmth, closeness, and nourishment. All we know is love, and regardless of its reciprocation, it is the elemental structure of our being. In these early stages, our minds have yet to be jaded by a complicated and unforgiving existence. Ego has not infiltrated our minds, and therefore our thoughts are unimpeded by the fear of human suffering or psychological pain. This love we feel—the love of the soul—is archetypal. It is present in each one of us, to some degree. Even as adults, when our love becomes buried under heaps of traumatic experience, it is still there, waiting to be uncovered. One of my most inspirational roles as a psychologist is to help my patients find it once more. But when it is rediscovered, love is often damaged or diluted. This is when love may become an addiction.

As Robert Palmer so aptly crooned in a 1985 megahit, *might as well face it, you're addicted to love.*[26] Love addiction is real and affects millions of people from all walks of life. In fact, I would argue that most relationships between romantic partners, family members, and close friends are hindered by an unhealthy concept of love. If only we could revert to the comprehension of love we held as babies—but this is challenging for most adults, as we are perpetually stuck in our egotistical thought process. For many adults, love is painful, conditional, and obsessive—three characteristics that the soul never intended it to be. In contrast, the pure love of the soul is meant to invoke joy, to be universally applied and without a sense of urgency. So, how have we strayed so far from the authentic tenets of our soul's love? Well, this is one of the prices of being human.

As we move from childhood to adolescence and into adulthood, we begin living in our heads and not our

---

26  Palmer, Robert, vocalist, "Addicted to Love," by Robert Palmer, track 3 on *Riptide*, Island Records, vinyl.

hearts. We place so much emphasis on the acquisition of facts and information and much less on the development of a healthy psyche. Our society deserves most of the blame for this, as emotional and mental health have not been historically prioritized on a cultural, policied, or legislative level. (One need only look at No Child Left Behind to see how standardized measurements superseded individual concern.)[27] Even if love is valued by parents or caregivers, it is usually not modeled by them in the healthiest ways. Our parents are human beings, and most of them have not effectively dealt with the wounds of their own childhoods. This left them unprepared to administer healthy love to their children and more likely to pass on the intergenerational trauma of a family system. How our parent(s) treat us is often somewhat determined by how they were treated by their parent(s). If there was a dearth of love in their household, they may be uncomfortable expressing it to us in the way we need. Most of the patients I have worked with recall feeling as though they did not receive enough love from their parents. This tale is common for the love addict who seeks validation and attention from partners to meet this childhood lack.

So what is a love addict, really? Remember that addiction is simply an obsessive surge of energy collected in our thoughts that leads us to compulsive action. With

27 United States. Congress (107th, 1st session : 2001). No Child Left Behind Act of 2001: Conference Report to Accompany H.R. 1. Washington: U.S. Government Printing Office, 2001.

love addiction, it is no different. The love addict has bought into the myth that a deep, committed, long-term relationship is the solution to their dissatisfaction with life. Thoughts about the perfect mate consume them, and they become obsessed with finding one. Dating apps are heaven for the love addict—scrolling left and right becomes a daily ritual. For the most part, the love addict falls hard and fast. Within a matter of a few encounters, they are certain that they have found the right person. They put their potential mates up on a pedestal almost immediately and see only the good in them, discounting anything that may not be ideal as well as the proverbial red flags. The love addict searches for the feeling of love as their savior—they believe that someone else is ultimately responsible for their sense of joy and it is only through the communal aspects of life that they will be fulfilled.

It is the compulsion of the love addict to constantly be in seeking mode. It becomes the dominant energetic force that drives their thoughts and actions. They are looking for something that perhaps they have never been able to find: a healthy, stable relationship that includes mutual affection and excitement. Unfortunately, the love addict tend to push too hard in their quest. Their timeline for love is short; they pursue it with desperation and urgency. Often, the recipients of this torrent of romantic neediness pull back from the intensity. Much to the dismay of the love addict, the more they express their powerful feelings, the more their potential partners have second thoughts. The recognition that your suitor is coming on too strong is actually a healthy one, but it does not feel that way to the love addict. The love addict can't understand why everyone doesn't feel the way they do and are perplexed when their new partners try to set boundaries and even break up with them. They feel victimized and misunderstood and their love remains unrequited, so they move on to the next available, unsuspecting mark.

The love addict is driven by a desire to be seen. It is often an unconscious force that drives them, and they feel powerless and resistant to change their behavior. The fairy tale of love becomes the central axis on which the love addict turns. The idea of love is much more compelling to them than the relationship itself, for they are moved by the will of the ego and not of the soul. The ego has grabbed hold of the idea that without romantic love, life is meaningless. Remember, the ego is powerful, misleading, and often toxic. It believes it has our best interests in mind, but more often than not it is propelled by fear. Fear is the polar opposite of love.

I am currently seeing a patient caught in the throes of love addiction. They are no stranger to Hinge, Match, and Bumble and joked that they should buy stock in all three. In the two years previous to our work together, they have been in love six times—or so they thought. Each relationship had ended after a few months, usually a few days after they had professed their devotion. They reluctantly admitted that they had been dumped by most of the boyfriends they'd ever had. When they met a guy they liked, they became overtaken by a desire to see him all the time. They couldn't control their need to text him on an hourly basis, and their mood depended wholly on the content of the replies they received. They tried to hold themselves back, but to no avail. They knew that their methodology was backfiring, that it was pushing men away, but they had no idea how to change the dysfunctional pattern that stuck to them like a shadow. They couldn't bear the thought of being single, because they believed that their happiness was contingent on being in love. Without a loving partner, they felt that their life would be meaningless. They hated being alone and thought it reflected their undesirability. They suffered from low self-esteem—a product of their family upbringing. I could tell that they had lost all contact with their soul. When I asked them about it, their response was "What soul?"

We have been working together to find it ever since. We discussed that it would be difficult to love someone else unless they began the process of loving themself first. We uncovered that they were looking for someone to save them from the arduous task of working out their own issues. For years, they had avoided the topic of themself—both dismissing it as selfish and being too frightened to dig into the emotional trauma of their past. Instead, they scanned the horizon for a shiny object— men mostly—that they perceived would rescue them. Unfortunately, their pain was far too cumbersome, and their insecurities surfaced almost immediately in every relationship. After working through some of their negative childhood beliefs and replacing them with more truthful and positive ones, we began to focus on the present. The question remained: How could they begin to love themself after so many years of self-doubt and diffidence? The answer was inside them all along. Their soul was waiting to heal them.

As a psychologist, I am aware that focusing on harmful beliefs created by family trauma is a vital way in which to heal. But there are also other effective methods to boost self-esteem and find self-love. The ego perpetuates limiting and detrimental thoughts that sometimes are difficult to shake. In some cases, it is best to take the focus off ourselves and focus more on the core values we have established. The soul is generous, kind, and thoughtful, and these attributes apply to your relationship not only with yourself, but also with others. Self-love is fostered by the esteemable actions we engage in as well as how we treat ourselves. In order to build self-esteem, sometimes we must look past ourselves and pivot toward others in need. Helping people who are less fortunate is congruent with the will of the soul. Here is an exercise that will make you feel better about who you are as a person.

**Exercise**
1. *This week, do something for someone else. This could be a friend of yours or even someone you do not know well. Think about something this person may need. It could be a ride home, a raise, or a soccer jersey for their child. Take initiative and approach this person with a kind gesture that is out of your normal comfort*

*zone. Make your gift something meaningful so they will feel an impact in their life. This does not have to be monetary but could simply be an hour of your time. Give something away with no questions asked. Here's the kicker: you're not allowed to tell anyone that you have done this. It's your secret. Many feel a rush of positive energy when they volunteer; donate their time, money, or needed good to a charitable organization; or get involved with a mutual aid group. That is the soul acknowledging your action.*

In the same way that love may become an addiction, the obsessive desire to quell our pain can lead to a sex addiction. Let me be clear—there is absolutely nothing wrong with having sex. Quite the contrary. Sex can be a wonderful expression of love, intimacy, and caring. As humans, we were built to have sex, and through this act we solidify bonds and procreate. Sex, in its pure and healthy form, is a gift that makes our lives brighter, happier, and more passionate. We are drawn to another not only through common interest and emotional energy but through our pheromones. However, when the mind is consumed by an impulse to have sex so constant that it becomes a driving force in our lives, we are caught in an addictive cycle similar to that of drugs and alcohol. Yes, sex is like a drug.

Sex addicts think about it all the time and attempt to manipulate their intimate relationships so that sex becomes the focus. They place a disproportionate value on the sexual experience, considering it to be the most vital part of a loving relationship. Sex makes them feel safe, loved, and validated in a manner that words and other actions cannot. Those addicted to sex do not want to be told they are wonderful or have an arm placed around their shoulder. Instead, they long for a salacious physical touch that eases their insecurity and allows them to feel connected to another.

The intense feeling of an orgasm is one of the most gratifying we may have as human beings. And those who are caught in the obsessive cycle of sexual compulsion chase this climax with reckless abandon. They fantasize about this moment of release and imagine themselves performing the act. Similar to heroin addicts haunted by thoughts of their next fix, the sex addict obsesses about the next sexual encounter and will go to great lengths to experience it. They hunt for others, often causing discomfort by placing so much emphasis on the sexual act. Sex addicts grow weary of partners who retract from their robust sexual appetite and move from one person to another to get their needs met. They have difficulty dropping into the emotional aspects of a relationship and feel rejected if their desires are not met. They judge themselves on the prowess of their performance, growing insecure if their physical passion is unrequited.

Many sex addicts begin using pornography as a way to satiate their incessant fixation. And with thousands of porn sites available and free on the internet, there is no stopping them once the obsession begins. Some sex addicts spend several hours per day watching porn and masturbating. They steal away from their cubicle at work to catch an X-rated glimpse on their phones in a locked bathroom stall. They watch porn while they sit in bed at night returning emails. Anyone who watches porn regularly, even if it's a few times per week, may be caught in the cycle. Per our working definition of addiction here—obsessive thoughts followed by a compulsive action—it is not the frequency that matters, it is the presence of that cyclical energy.

Sex addicts who constantly watch porn, go to strip clubs, or visit prostitutes (all three are more prevalent than one would imagine) may develop an unrealistic vision of sexual intimacy. They grow attached to a fantasy or the thrill of these forbidden ventures. These become the stimuli on which their arousal depends, and this often dampens their sex lives outside the fantasy zone—where bodies are not airbrushed or lit for close-ups and there is no money exchanged.

When they try to have sex under normal circumstances, they often cannot perform. Some men suffer from erectile dysfunction for this very reason. They attempt to practice euphoric recall in bed (remembering an image that vivifies them) in order to maintain an erection. Sex no longer represents an act of love, but one of self-serving pleasure.

I have spoken with many people who have done the hard work of shedding their addiction to chemicals and other substances, only to face the emergence of this energy in a new form—the incessant desire for sexual consummation. As I have mentioned earlier, the obsessive/compulsive loop of addictive thoughts and actions has the ability to move from one idea to another. In fact, it has a propensity to devour whatever is in front of it, without hesitation, without bias. Much like food or exercise, sex is an integral part of our adult lives. If we abstained from food, we would die, and our bodies would atrophy if we stayed completely still. When we have an unhealthy relationship with these things, we cannot just give them up as we do with alcohol and drugs. So addressing these cravings—sex being at the top of the list—becomes more complicated and exacting. We do not want to give sex up altogether, as it is embedded in our nature and may keep the passion in our relationship. Instead of addressing the sex itself, we must go deeper and recalibrate our connection with ourselves. It is only through self-love that sexual addiction will heal.

Most sex addicts wear the guilt and shame of their misdeeds like a heavy cloak. They vow to change their ways after every encounter, but the thoughts return, and they are incapable of fending them off. This shame leads to depression, low self-esteem, frustration, and inaction. This is where forgiveness is essential as a tool for healing. The ego has taken hold of the addict, and now it is time to reintroduce the soul.

One of the most intrinsic qualities of the soul is the ability to forgive. Forgiveness is a healing gesture that allows us to expel harmful thoughts, beliefs, judgments, and resentments toward others. It reminds us of the compassion and empathy that reside in all of us, a universal language that we all share. Forgiveness has the power to break down defenses that have been holding us back from experiencing our true potential. It is the release of toxic energy and a shift toward a new more spiritual perspective. Forgiveness is available to each one of us—it is free and without limitations. Most of us were taught how to forgive others by our parents and teachers, but the importance of forgiving *ourselves* was not duly emphasized. Through self-forgiveness, we may find the path toward self-love. Forgiving ourselves is a tenet of the soul.

So, what does it really mean to forgive yourself? As you know, humans are an imperfect species full of contradictions, negative thoughts, false beliefs, envy, shame, and judgment. These harmful aspects of our humanity are present when we are ego-attached and view the world as an unfair place. We have been led to believe that comparison, competition, and criticism are healthy, as they push us forward to reach our goals. But the soul knows better. The soul wants you to forgive yourself. We have all made terrible decisions, acted out of fear, broken our promises, hurt others with our words or actions, blamed others for our misfortune. The reset button is waiting in your psyche, and you may press it at any time. Before you can love yourself, you need to forgive yourself. Before you can love someone else, you must first love yourself.

Self-forgiveness does not absolve you of your misdeeds in the past. It is not a get-out-of-jail-free card. If you have done bad things, you must be accountable and accept the consequences. Do not shy away from admission of your faulty behavior, as doing so is gesture of dishonesty. You are soul-aligned now, and this means you strive to live within the confines of your core values. You know that hurting others is not an authentic part of your being.

Affirmations are one of my favorite healing tools. They are positive self-statements that actually have the ability to change the chemistry in your brain. Much of the time, our negative thoughts override our ability to hear the truth—it is much easier to believe the false narrative in our minds. Affirmations help us find the truth again and replace the old tape running in our brains with a new, more accurate one. If we approach the mind with love and understanding, it can bend, modify, and reshape itself. Thus, our ego-driven self-talk can be overcome by the narrative of our soul. This affirmation is not only for self-forgiveness, but a pledge for you to align with the soul and change your behavior. You deserve this. You have suffered enough. Time to begin the process.

**Exercise**
**Affirmations—Self-Forgiveness**
*When you get up in the morning, find a quiet place where you can look at yourself in the mirror. This will be a five-minute exercise, so make sure you have found a secluded spot where no one will interrupt you. Power down your phone. Look at your reflection in the mirror and focus on your eyes. Then repeat these statements three times slowly.*

*I forgive myself today.*
*I forgive myself completely.*
*I forgive myself for the things I have done that I'm not proud of.*
*I will live differently today and align with my core values.*
*I forgive myself for being dishonest.*
*I will move away from old patterns that no longer serve me.*
*I forgive myself for being afraid.*
*I am no longer afraid of reaching my potential.*
*I forgive myself for making bad choices.*
*I will let my soul show me another way.*
*I forgive myself for feeling guilty and ashamed.*
*I will tell the truth about who I am and ask for help.*
*I forgive myself for judging myself and others.*
*I forgive myself for the decisions I've made that hurt others.*
*I forgive myself for being selfish and defensive.*
*As I forgive myself, I feel the negative energy leaving my body.*
*As I forgive myself, I feel my mind clear.*
*I am not perfect, nor do I want to be.*
*I will begin to love myself today.*
*I will love all my faults and imperfections.*
*I will love all my strengths and attributes.*
*When I forgive myself, I love myself.*
*When I love myself, I am connected to my soul.*
*When I am connected to my soul, I feel happy and free.*

*I deserve to be happy.*
*I deserve love.*

Affirmations have had a profound impact on my life. Uttering these words aloud will bring a new understanding and intention into consciousness. You may not believe the words at first, but don't doubt the alchemy of your imagination. Soon you will feel a shift in your psyche and begin to think of yourself in a different, more truthful manner. These affirmations will help you replace your old false narrative with a more accurate one. This is the will of the soul.

# 9 | EATING AND NOT EATING

One morning, when I looked in the mirror, I didn't like what I saw. There was something off, something wrong. In all my twelve years of life, I had never really thought about it before—the way I looked. I was a happy preteen who loved to play baseball and collect old beer cans, hated taking baths, and wore dirty clothes whenever I could. But something had changed overnight. It was as if someone had found me in my sleep and whispered terrible things into my ear. It was a strange and unfamiliar feeling, and it confused me. I tried, but there seemed like no way to silence the voices in my head. One dominant thought continued in a loop: "You don't look like yourself."

I went off to school feeling like a completely different

version of myself. Usually jovial and loquacious, I sat in the back of the class and said nothing. *Is someone playing a mean trick on me? Did something happen?* I scoured the logical regions of my brain but could find no answers. I prayed for the feeling to go away, but it didn't. When I got home and peered at myself in the hall mirror, it got louder. "You don't look like yourself." I had never faced a challenge that I could not overcome. I was resourceful and smart, at least according to my teachers. *Maybe if I change my appearance, I will feel comfortable again?* My haircut seemed okay—the same barber down the block had been cutting it for years, and no one had teased me about it at school. As I gazed into the mirror, I moved down from my hair and onto my face. Yes, there it was. There was something bothersome about my face. It was my cheeks—they were so round and chubby. I looked kind of like a chipmunk. *How can I ever walk out of the house again? Why hasn't anyone told me about this?* I pulled the skin on my cheeks tight and pushed it toward my ears. *Now that's the face I want to have.*

I soon made the connection that restricting the amount of food I put into my body would diminish the size of my cheeks. I started small—eating two cookies after school instead of four, giving up dessert after dinner. No one noticed. I was in complete control. But the results I wanted weren't happening fast enough, so I began to take more drastic measures. I only took a few bites of my cereal at breakfast, had a piece of bread at lunch, and ate only meat for dinner. My mother, father, and brother were too busy with their own stuff to notice. Or maybe they didn't care. I was getting away with it, and my face was shrinking. So was my body. My pants became loose around my waist, so I cinched them tight with an old belt. My shirts became baggy, so I tucked them in. Every morning I looked at myself in the mirror and was happier than the day before, but there was more to do—a lot more.

No breakfast, bread for lunch, chicken for dinner. No candy or cookies. No milk. No excuses. No exceptions. I could see my cheekbones now, and my ribs. *This is who I am supposed to be. This is handsome. This is cool.* And it was mine, all mine—no one could take this away from me. I was in charge of my body, and nobody could tell me what to do anymore.

I started feeling tired all the time. Baseball was one of my favorite activities, but my glove felt like a heavy stone, and my legs could hardly propel me down the field. When I woke up in the morning, I felt tired, exhausted even, and I fantasized about staying in bed forever. I fell asleep in class a few times. The school contacted my parents. This is when they became aware that something was amiss. But they still didn't notice that my body had grown smaller. So the trend continued for almost a year, until I became too weak to do anything. Finally, I was brought to the doctor, and the jig was up. He told my mother that I was twenty pounds underweight and probably anorexic. I was ashamed at being found out, but I still was happy with my appearance. I didn't want to change it for anyone.

My parents began monitoring my food intake, preparing high-calorie meals for me and watching me eat. They were embarrassed most of all. They had no idea why I would be starving myself. At the time, I didn't, either, but one thing was clear—it felt good. Around this time, I realized that I could eat as much food as I wanted and simply purge it into the toilet in the bathroom. No one told me how to do this—I had never heard about bulimia. It just came naturally to me. I would eat what they wanted me to eat, swiftly excuse myself at the end of the meal, and empty my stomach. I gained a bit of weight back, enough to satisfy them and call off the dogs, and my life returned to normal. "Normal" became a constant deception that consumed me for the next ten years. Throughout high school and college, I remained bulimic. My eating disorders were my first experience with a serious addictive cycle.

My obsession centered on controlling exactly how I looked, and through the vehicle of restricting and purging my food intake, I became an expert at this. My compulsive behavior was monitoring the calories I consumed, checking my weight on the bathroom scale, fixating on my physical appearance, and purging my food after eating. Here again, we see the loop of obsessive thoughts and compulsive actions. So, how did this addictive cycle suddenly take hold of me at such a young age? Out of all the kids in my seventh-grade class, why was I the only one with an eating disorder?.

During the early years of this self-destructive pattern,

I wasn't really aware that my thoughts and actions were problematic. Other than feeling sluggish and detached, my life continued in a fairly typical way. I had friends, girlfriends, did well in school, played sports, and experimented with drugs. But no drug could get me as high as the process of purging my system, which stimulated something in my brain and filled me with euphoria. I would come out of the bathroom feeling confident, settled, calm, and charismatic. I actually felt stoned for a while, as the act of throwing up sent a rush of dopamine into my neurological receptors. I got used to this feeling and embraced it as a way to counter my insecurity and sadness—the real causes of my dysfunctional relationship with food.

When I was eleven years old, the yelling began to intensify in my house. My father, who was gone most of the time on business trips, would storm around and rage at my mother. I would huddle outside their bedroom door and listen intently to the insults that flew. It became commonplace to see them argue, and in her increasing despair, my mother began to drink heavily. When my father was away, she relied on me to listen to her sad stories. My dad was cheating on her, having affairs all over town, and she couldn't understand why. She asked if I knew the answer—an inappropriate question for her eleven-year-old son. I tried to console her as often as I could, but her behavior became more erratic and vengeful. After a few years of constant tumult, my father left for good, taking my brother—my best friend—to live with him. My family was splintering apart, and there was nothing I could do to prevent it. Everything seemed out of control.

As with many who suffer the grueling entanglement with eating disorders, mine stemmed from a need for control. I know this now. But during my ten-year bout with them, I could not pinpoint their origin. Hindsight, of course, is twenty-twenty, especially with an adult perspective enhanced by advanced degrees in psychology. Insidious as it may seem, my sovereignty over the way I nourished my body was the only authority I had back then. For everything else, I was reliant on a family system that was failing me terribly. The ground underneath my feet was constantly shifting. How the disorder evolved is still a mystery—why did I choose food? Even to this day, I am perplexed by this question, but it may revolve around the immediate and accessible nature of it. I believed, at that fragile moment in time, that safety meant counting on my secretive behavior. I found solace in holding this thing that was uniquely my own, that I could manipulate without permission. I had no other secrets, really, and this one was a layer of protection that no one could remove.

The trauma of my parents' fighting brought a new type of fear into my life. I became consumed with the idea that they were headed for divorce; it was inconceivable, this notion of fracture. And yet there it was, staring me in the face. I tried to imagine what this would be like, separate camps and families—but my parents had always projected this promise that we would be together forever. What a bunch of bullshit. The promise was now shattered into a million pieces, and I receded inward to fend for myself—my survival was on the line. I had always liked myself, but in the midst of all this grief, I didn't recognize my face anymore. This is when the addiction slipped in.

My story is not unique—there are lots of children who come from broken homes. But the way in which I soothed myself is fairly uncommon. Eating disorders do not infiltrate the psyche of many adolescents. Other disorders, such as anxiety, extreme defiance, anger issues, and emotional dysregulation, are more prevalent. When children experience emotional trauma, such as a heated divorce, fear and confusion remove them from a path toward the soul and instead empower the harmful influence of ego. They suddenly suffer misgivings about their own place in the world and feel as though something has been stolen from them. And it has—their innocence. It is nearly impossible to restore it. This is what prompts children to begin acting in a way that is out of character.

Many of the adults who develop eating disorders are also responding to unresolved emotional trauma from their own childhood experiences that have been suppressed.[28] But as I discussed in Chapter Four, there is also a lot of social pressure to look a certain way in

---

28 María F. Rabito-Alcón, José I. Baile, and Johan Vanderlinden, "Mediating Factors between Childhood Traumatic Experiences and Eating Disorders Development: A Systematic Review," *Children* 8, no. 2 (June 2021): p. 114, https://doi.org/10.3390/children8020114.

the modern world, and we are bombarded with more images than ever before in history. In my lifetime, the prevailing idea has been that a thin body is an attractive body—even going so far as "heroin chic" becoming all the rage in the mid-1990s. Social media, with its filters and apps like Facetune, and traditional media, with Photoshop and airbrushing, set the trends—even though some looks are physical impossibilities. For many of us, our weight is a perpetual concern that ultimately leads to negative thoughts and self-judgment. We obsess about how much we weigh and whether or not our jeans are too tight.

Dieting has become so pervasive in the US that it is a billion-dollar enterprise. There are all types of diet pills, powders, supplements, meal-delivery services, calorie-counting programs, retreats, fat transfers, liposuction technologies, fat-freezing methods...and the list goes on. Celebrities smile at us from the TV with their personal tales of shedding the evil fat cells from their bodies. This is more than just a fad or a trend—it has become an archetypal storyline. I imagine that most of you have been on a diet at one point in your life. And you know how it feels when you see others restricting their caloric intake or depriving themselves of foods they cherish. You empathize with them and understand the urgency with which they proceed. You have internalized the message that *thinner is more desirable, more acceptable* and that you will receive more attention and opportunity if your waistline is cinched. Sadly, this is often true, as fatphobia does exist.

Juxtaposed to the tendency we have to restrict our consumption, there is also an obesity epidemic plaguing America.[29] This is partly the result of processed and fatty foods that are available and less expensive than healthier options. Fast food restaurants are an example of this—it is astounding how many people eat at them multiple times per week. But obesity may also be a genetic condition or the manifestation of unprocessed emotional trauma. Some of us self-medicate with food in the same way a person with alcohol-use disorder turns to the bottle. It soothes our negative emotions—anger, fear, sadness, shame—while wreaking havoc on the body. Food distracts us from the psychological anguish, like swallowing a painkiller, but our unmetabolized feelings rise to the surface again. Not only does the body suffer from the condition of obesity, but it holds a social stigma that often leads to ostracization and judgment. Much like starving oneself, the patterns of obsessive thought and compulsive action characterized by overeating land squarely within the parameters of addiction.

Many Americans have an unhealthy relationship with food. As a culture, we eat either too much or not enough. We depend on food for sustenance and strength but, for some, it taunts us, calls to us—gives us no peace.

---

29  As of this writing, according to the most recent report provided by the Centers for Disease Control, 42.4 percent of adults had obesity and 9.2 percent had severe obesity in 2017, the highest rate ever recorded in the U.S. CDC. "Adult Obesity Facts." Centers for Disease Control and Prevention, September 30, 2021. https://www.cdc.gov/obesity/data/adult.html.

We just cannot let the last chocolate chip cookie stay in the jar—it's just not possible. I have heard of people padlocking their fridge at night to avoid the temptation of the midnight snack. The urge is so powerful that they consider going into the garage and getting the bolt cutters. This is addict behavior.

So, what is a healthy relationship to food, anyway? This is something I had to learn after a decade of malnourishment. I have come to understand that the food we put into our bodies is a reflection of how we feel about ourselves. When we are balanced and healthy psychologically, our alliance with food becomes one of trust and respect. Food does not hold us captive when we exhibit self-love. A healthy relationship with food is one of appreciation, exploration, and curiosity. Food should never create insecurity, fear of any sort, low self-esteem, or pathology. It is one of our most vital and delicious assets and should be embraced as the essential ingredient to our well-being that it can be.

When we think of food—breads, pastries, vegetables, pastas, soufflés, sauces, cheeses, berries, leafy greens, prime rib, baked potatoes—we should smile and be thankful for our taste buds. But a healthy attitude toward food moves beyond reverence—it must extend further to a personal exploration of how our bodies respond to it. Sugar makes some of us jumpy, caffeine may keep us up at night, pasta and bread may stop us up, and green beans may give us gas. Each one of our complicated physiological biospheres are completely unique and therefore require personal attention. Learn what foods agree with your system, read about the foods you love, educate yourself about the nutrients and vitamins you need for longevity. There is so much literature out there—find the experts whose outlook suits you, but only ones who encourage eating, not dieting or restricting. Preparing and eating food is one of the great pleasures of being human—it is also one we cannot do without. So, how do we dispel the anxiety we feel about it? Well, it begins with grounding ourselves in our bodies and listening for the soul.

The soul wants you to know peace. The soul does not want you to restrict yourself or overindulge—it wants to help you find the sweet spot where we are balanced. Where our nourished bodies can thrive, free from the need of the ego, which can never be sated. If the thoughts in your mind are stuck in ego, place your right hand over your heart. Listen carefully for the drumbeat of your pulse and imagine how hard your heart is working to keep you alive. This is how hard your soul is working as well. Remember, your soul will emerge with resounding acclamation if you acknowledge its existence. Time to check in.

**Exercise**
*On a daily basis, we collect negative thoughts and harmful beliefs as well as toxic energy from the chemicals and electromagnetic frequencies that surround us. One of the most effective ways to release these from our physical bodies and our minds is to take off our shoes and connect our bare feet to the earth. This process is*

called earthing and is one of the healthiest and most replenishing rituals that exist. It is a way to connect deeply with your soul and attach yourself to the soul of the earth. The soul of the earth is the most powerful energy that exists to us and will cleanse your body and mind completely.

Earthing is a way to become grounded in the body. It reconnects our body to the natural polarities of the earth and rebalances our nervous system. It relieves the stress, blockages, and trauma that are stored in our cells. Your body will align into its natural posture as you walk in bare feet. You will feel a different relationship with your body—stronger and more vital. This is the way we walked the earth for thousands of years before shoes existed. You will feel a freedom from the limitations and constrictions of your body as you begin to walk.

There are a few ways to proceed. I have the benefit of living in a mountainous region that is also close to the ocean. For forty-five minutes per day, I hike on a trail or walk on the beach with my bare feet touching the earth. If you do not have access to these luxuries, you simply need a patch of grass or dirt—perhaps in your garden or a nearby park. Sitting down on a blanket with the bottoms of your bare feet touching the ground is also perfect. Power down your phone. Relax. Enjoy this moment.

When you are walking or sitting, imagine all the energy that does not belong to you passing through your body and releasing from the bottoms of your feet into the ground. Repeat these words.

*I ask you, my soul, to clear my body and mind of all
negativity.*

*Help me, my soul, to release my harmful thoughts
and limiting beliefs into the earth.*

*I ask you, my soul, to release my ego into the earth
so I may be aligned with you.*

*Remind me, my soul, of the beauty that resides
within me.*

*Teach me, my soul, to love myself with the nourish-
ment of healthy food.*

*Affirm in me, my soul, that eating healthy food is an
expression of love.*

*Show me, my soul, how to accept my physical body
with grace and admiration.*

*I ask you, my soul, to connect with the soul of
Mother Earth.*

*I ask you, Mother Earth, to take away my negativ-
ity.*

*I ask you, Mother Earth, to fill me with your power-
ful healing energy.*

*I ask you, Mother Earth, to replenish my body with
your minerals, vitamins, and ions.*

*I ask you, Mother Earth, to pass your wisdom into
my mind.*

*I am grateful, Mother Earth, for your kindness and
support.*

# 10 ) WORK AND SUCCESS

From our earliest moments, we seek feedback from our primary caregivers for achieving certain milestones—smiling for the first time, taking our first steps, learning to use the toilet, walking down the stairs, and so on. When we receive praise for these accomplishments, it affirms a belief in us that we are capable and appreciated. Instinctively, we already know this, as we are more aligned with our souls during childhood, but few things are better than a big smile from our human caregivers. By the time we're in school, we are ranked by our ability to follow directions, recite information, and use problem-solving skills. Our primary caregivers' perception of how we are doing is influenced partially by the messaging they receive from school. So, a better report card often translates to a happier set of primary caregivers, while a negative report is cause for concern. We are pushed by our teachers to excel in different subjects, and when we exceed expectations, we are praised, much like the adulation we crave from our primary caregivers. But when we struggle and disengage, the treatment we receive is quite different.

Many schools place undue emphasis on scholastic development and less on the emotional and spiritual elements of the psyche. This was the case in my upbringing. I was instructed that academic prowess was far more important than the cultivation of the self. Therefore, I believed that good grades were the keys to happiness. My parents reinforced this at home, showering me with privileges when I brought home A's and punishing me if they thought I was underperforming. My first real understanding of success was an alphabetic letter—a written symbol of my overall worth. I was also taught that winning in games or sports was success and losing was failure. I began judging myself by these standards.

Among my peers in high school, acceptance into a good college was considered the crown jewel of our young careers. We packed our applications with standardized testing scores, extracurricular activities, athletics, recommendations, and grade point averages— then offered them up to the gods of higher education admissions. There was tremendous pressure placed on excellence, and any youthful infractions might lead to the unthinkable: rejection from the school of your choice. This was exactly my experience. I was rejected by most of the colleges I applied to, and much to my parents' dismay, I shuffled myself off to a less prestigious institution. In their eyes, it was a failure, and I had been conditioned to see things through their eyes. I had let them down. I had let myself down. I had botched my future.

Why? Because the better the college, the better the job. The better the job, the more money earned. The more money earned, the happier the life. Money means success . . . right?

In 1990, I left college. I was unhappy with the repetitiveness of my daily routine and longed for a change. Armed with a backpack, a change of clothes, leather boots, and a canteen, I boarded a plane bound for Asia with two of my best friends. After a few months of meandering, we wound up on a hiking trail in the foothills of Nepal. I was twenty years old at the time and a fairly seasoned traveler, but I had never encountered such beauty as this. We began a three-week trek in the Himalayas. With each passing day, I became more aware that the energy in these revered mountains was radically different from that of the cities and towns I knew in North America. There was a purity in the air that sparked a sense of freedom in us we had never known. And the Nepalese people were unlike anyone we had met in our sheltered and privileged lives.

A week into the journey, we stumbled upon a town—a gathering of a few traditional farmhouses and a temple. We stayed for the night in a stone structure without windows or electricity, heated only by the stove that also cooked our meals. There was no television, radio, or technology of any kind—only the companionship of the owner and his family to keep us occupied. I was astounded by their kindness and generosity and the simplicity with which they lived. I remember thinking to myself, *these are the happiest people on earth.* They were full of smiles, laughter, and loving gestures delivered with total sincerity. Their clothes had been sewn by them, their house built by them, and the food was grown by them. They had rarely left the small plot of land they so carefully farmed, because all their needs were met, entirely. It was evident that the outside world was foreign to them, and they had no intention of exploring it. They basked in utter contentment and spoke only of their good fortune. Spending the night with them changed my view of the world. I wanted what they had—but had no clue how to get there.

As with the end of all vacations, the transition back to reality was turbulent, especially reintegrating into Western culture after six months of exploring. I wanted to go back to that town every day, but I was pulled by enrollment, responsibilities, and the internalized message that graduating from college meant a job, money, and success. So I turned my back on the soul and, as usual, let the ego lead. And fear came with it. Fear of failure, fear of letting my parents down, fear of being different. This fear led to a diploma that I didn't really want and a job in New York City.

Many people do not care for their jobs. This is unfortunate, as so much time and energy are spent doing them. Love the job or hate it, the possibility of slipping into an addictive cycle remains. Addiction to work is often perpetuated by fear and low self-esteem—both products of the ego. So many of us become fixated on the idea that our ascension up the corporate ladder will remove our self-doubt and insecurity. The correlation between achievement and worthiness leads us to believe that a job defines who one is as a person. By this logic, the more you rise through the ranks, the more evolved you become. Frequently, one's self-worth becomes interwoven with one's stature in the work environment. Therefore, if you are not excelling in the office, you may feel poorly about yourself as a whole. A demotion or loss of a job may be devastating to your self-esteem, and this pushes the ego into overdrive in an attempt to protect itself from shame.

Work addiction is marked by a constant stream of obsessive thoughts about your job, usually driven by fear, that may only be quelled through the act of toil. The mental chatter will not cease until you sit down at the computer or take out the phone. The thoughts become so invasive that they prevent you from being present with the other pressing circumstances of your life. Marriages fail, relationships with children suffer, friends fall to the wayside, anxiety crescendos. This obsessive and compulsive loop is a home-wrecker, as work addicts prioritize their vocation over everything else. They cannot help themselves. In America, and Western culture in general, the signal is clear—wealth and power are noble objectives. If you grasp them, you will inherit the keys to the kingdom of happiness. But as anyone who has chased wealth and power will tell you, there is no finish line. We yearn to find the end of the rainbow, but as we approach, it disappears. It is a self-perpetuating myth that intoxicates us with greed—as we collect titles, raises, and influence, we simply want more.

A significant portion of my patients have amassed considerable wealth, whether through inheritance or innovation and hard work. I have treated CEOs of Fortune 500 companies, founders of well-known tech start-ups, celebrated entrepreneurs and business owners. These patients have sought my guidance for several different reasons, but they share a commonality that is undeniable—their so-called success has not brought them love, serenity, or self-respect. Quite the contrary—it has often contributed to feelings of disillusionment, mistrust, and loneliness. On the balance sheet, they have surpassed their own expectations, but emotionally, they have continued to fall short. I've heard it more than once: "I've worked so hard all my life, and I'm just not happy."

That money equals happiness and success is such a fallacy that it seems laughable, but we are fed this equation from the beginning, so how could we doubt it? I was infected by this narrative for much of my life until I realized I was living in someone else's story, not my own. Since then, I have grappled with this question—what does "success" really mean?

According to the soul, the basic information that

we have obtained about success is false. It is a trick of the ego that the meaning of life is the attainment of stature, money, or fancy job titles. Most of us who have achieved these can refute this. The soul does not care about the size of your bank account. It is not concerned with your job title, promotability, or level of influence around the office cooler. Your soul does not think this way, not at all. For the soul, success is determined by thoughts in the mind, emotions in the psyche, and feelings in the body. The soul is crystal clear in its messaging that your identity is solely elevated by your adherence to spiritual principles. These principles include honesty, integrity, passion, excitement, and optimism. For example, if you have fostered an environment of goodwill, generosity, and kindness in your career, your soul will reward you with a sense of calmness and fulfillment. Falling prey to the avarice and self-centeredness of the workplace will ultimately lead to suffering and psychological discord.

When we prioritize the needs of the ego, fear, frustration, and guilt will loom large in our psyche. This may manifest in the form of nagging, anxious thoughts about the future, regret about the past, low frustration tolerance, and general dissatisfaction with your circumstances. I imagine that most of us know well these ego-based feelings that follow us around like a malevolent shadow. But remember, this is not our natural state of being. This emotional discomfort signals that we are off track. It is the soul trying to tell us that we are heading in the wrong direction—toward ego.

I ask my patients, "How do you feel when you are lying in bed, about to go to sleep? What do you reflect upon in these moments?" The answer is often negative. In these still moments, before dozing off, most people are afraid. How could that be considered success? With all the resources at their disposal, with all the accolades and education, with all the effort—they are still filled with anxiety and fear. This has become my litmus test for success—how do you feel when you are alone, before sleep, with your head on the pillow?

During these precious minutes before slumber, a successful person should feel a sense of peace. There should be no despair, worry, or resentment. There should be joyful musing about the day marked by gratitude and appreciation. As always, the soul is awaiting your embrace. Success has been misconstrued in a way that pushes the ego to take inventory—in complete opposition to the essence of the soul. The soul asks you simply to accept all your parts, good and bad, with an attitude of nonjudgment. When you are aligned with the soul, you are naturally and organically successful. Have you ever met someone who has very little in the way of possessions or money but who radiates a frequency of kindness and satisfaction? This person has heard the voice of the soul and found allegiance with it. In the opinion of the soul, this person is a success—just like the family in the Himalayan village. Meeting them was my first encounter with people in complete alignment with their souls. I couldn't articulate this back then, but in hindsight it has become abundantly clear. Their souls were dominant, and ego was nowhere to be found.

The soul wants you to stop and smell the roses—figuratively and literally. Your soul wants you to know that with or without a job, you are still a beautiful person—that a job in no way defines your character. The soul asks you to have integrity in all your interactions with others and yourself. The concept of integrity includes all your pursuits, not only those designated by your boss. This is not to say that whatever work you do is meaningless or without merit. Rather, we are trying to assess whether addictive forces are at play. Ask yourself these questions:

1. *Have I broken promises to my children because of work?*
2. *Have I ruined romantic relationships because of work?*
3. *Have I neglected the activities I love because of work?*
4. *Am I constantly thinking about work and unable to focus on other things?*
5. *Do the thoughts go away only when I engage with work?*

If you have answered *yes* to any of these, you may be caught in an addictive cycle.

One of the most deliberate and effective ways I have discovered to access the soul is through the breath. This has been a spiritual practice employed by several different cultures for thousands of years. The simple act of taking a breath can give us pause from the voracious need of the ego and allow us to relax, go inward, and be present with our surroundings. Throughout my journey, I have always been aware that controlling my breathing has the ability to transform my thoughts. A few deep breaths as a remedy to frustration have cleared my mind of negativity and emotional discomfort on many occasions. Anxiety and spite are no match for the breath. Breathing intentionally is a direct conduit to the soul.

In 2005, I explored a nontraditional type of therapy called holotropic breathwork—a practice developed by psychiatrist Stanislav Grof in the 1970s.[30] This was the first time I met my soul and witnessed it in its tangible form. Through a methodical type of circular breathing, I entered into a nonordinary state of consciousness that opened up the passageway to my authentic being. And when I arrived in front of it, I was not afraid. My soul presented itself as a golden orb of concentrated light, like my own personal sun, and it spoke to me with words I will never forget. *You do not have to suffer anymore,* it said. *I am your inner light, and I have always been here to protect you. I will always be here and will never leave you alone. You have forgotten me, and I am here now to remind you that you are love. You are whole.*

---

30  Grof, Stanislav, Grof, Christina. *Holotropic Breathwork: A New Approach to Self-Exploration and Therapy.* United States: State University of New York Press, 2010.

*You are complete. You do not need to search anymore. You have found yourself. We are the same. Never forget this again.*

As you might imagine, I wept uncontrollably as I heard this kind voice speaking from the light. In that moment, all the shame and guilt released from my mind, and I was reminded that I was good. Over the next year, I returned for several more sessions and continued my conversation with my soul. This is a practice that is accessible to you as well. There are Grof-trained practitioners who teach holotropic breathwork all over the world. I highly recommend it.

## Exercise

*Here is another type of breath exercise that will connect you with the soul. It will help to quiet the mind and dissolve the ego, giving you a sense of peace and neutrality. Sit with your spine aligned as best you can. Kneel or sit cross-legged or in a chair with your hips and spine supported. Turn your palms facedown on your thighs. Close your eyes. Inhale and exhale through the nose. This is a five-minute exercise.*

*Inhale for four seconds.*

*When you inhale, feel the natural expansion of the ribs and lungs while the diaphragm drops down and widens into the belly. Think about kindness, generosity, expansion, and belief filling your body and your mind. These are the true markers of success.*

*Hold for four seconds. Feel your eyes releasing*

*toward the back of the brain, collarbones stretching wide.*

*Exhale for six seconds.*

*When you exhale, release out of the crown of the head, allowing the spine to rise and maintain its true alignment. Imagine all your ambition, insecurity, mistrust, and greed flowing out of your mind and your body. These emotions are from an old paradigm that no longer serves you.*

*Hold for two seconds. Explore the feeling of emptiness in the lungs.*

*You are now aligned with your soul.*

Remember, it is how you feel when you are lying in bed at night that determines your level of success. If you are worried, resentful, unhappy, or ashamed, you are not a success—just yet, anyway. But you can get there if you want. If you feel warm, hopeful, safe, thankful, and calm, you are a success, in my opinion. Because what good are the accolades if you don't feel you deserve them?

# 11 | EXAGGERATION AND LIES

In 2005, I was arrested for two DUIs in less than twelve months. I was facing jail time and was terrified that I would lose everything. As part of the legal process, I was forced to take a psychological evaluation that would, according to the district attorney's office in Albuquerque, New Mexico, determine whether I was telling the truth about the incident. The test was comprised of one hundred questions—some easy, others more ambiguous—that were designed to determine the level of reliability in my statements. Being a graduate student in psychology at the time, I was well aware of the snare traps laid carefully among the more innocuous questions. I suspected that if I lied on the exam, I would likely go to jail, so I proceeded with caution.

On the first page, there was a true-or-false question that asked me whether "I tell the truth all the time." My immediate impulse was to answer that of course this was true, but after I pondered for a moment, I concluded that it was false. Even though I held honesty in high regard, I was not a saint and sometimes said things that were untrue. On the second page came "I never lie," which was the same sentiment as before hidden in different language. This was also false. It felt strange to incriminate myself on a document that held my fate on its pages, but in this instance, I knew that I had to be completely truthful. In other situations, without the threat of incarceration, I may have answered differently.

Most of us claim honesty as one of our core values. We say that we are *honest* people, but are we really? Do you always tell the truth? If I were to ask you that right now, would you say yes? "Yes" would likely be a lie. For most of us, a more appropriate answer would be "I try to, whenever possible, but not always." So, why is it so difficult to be honest about our honesty? If it's a flaw that we all share, an archetypal human trait, why do our falsehoods fill us with guilt and self-judgment? Perhaps we consider our lying a character flaw. Perhaps our reaction stems from our intuition— the deep voice inside that calibrates our moral compass. Honesty *is* a tenet of the soul, and when we are less than honest, the soul does take notice. Remember, the soul witnesses your transgressions but will always accept you completely, no matter what you have done.

The truth is that most of us lie frequently. Even

when we don't intend to, we stretch the truth anyway. We manipulate our tax returns, tell people we love them when we don't, inflate our accomplishments with hyperbole, and respond to people's questions erroneously. Sometimes we do this without thinking—if the phone wakes you up and you hear on the other end, "Oh, I'm sorry, are you sleeping?" for some reason our programmed response is, "No, not at all, I'm wide-awake!" Why would we lie about something as mundane as sleep, something everyone does? We all doze off, and we all know that sleep is integral to our health. Yet we feel compelled to lie about it, as though it is an admission of weakness or immaturity to doze off.

Sometimes our lies are so inconsequential that it's as if they didn't happen. Others are bigger, maybe harmful to others. We may lie to prevent someone from having hurt feelings. When they ask if we like their outfit, we respond with a yes and swallow our real opinion (absolutely hideous!). Is this really so bad, if it's in the service of protecting a person's fragile self-esteem? And we lie to protect our own, as well. We fear judgment and create a false reality in order to prop ourselves up—something as simple as stating we have read a certain book, when we have not. Have you ever said, "I'm doing fine" after someone asks how you are—though you're far from fine? Instead of letting someone in, this common little lie erects a wall of protection that fortifies a projection of self. Unfortunately, the projection is artificial.

So, why do we fabricate these narratives when

our fundamental authentic nature proposes just the opposite? Well, once again we must grapple with the vastness of ego. The ego strives to conjure a self-image that it perceives as secure, preventing vulnerability from emerging. The ego lives in fear and constantly assesses the psychological safety of every situation. It reacts in a nanosecond and fashions its responses out of self-preservation. The ego believes that in order to be loved, we must be a certain way. This understanding is reinforced by the rejection, abandonment, and criticism all humans experience to some degree. We are dishonest when we are ego-attached, which for most of us is every day. No, I'm not calling you a liar; rather, I am stating that the ego's most effective defense mechanism is to deceive.

This has been on display for decades in the political sphere. It is not uncommon for politicians to distort reality. Unfortunately, a culture of dishonesty often shrouds the hallowed halls of Washington, D.C. In many cases, there is a clash of "facts" that oppose one another in the media, presenting the exact same events in juxtaposition. While this is nothing new, the rhetoric has risen to new levels of division and hostility. When we talk about the harm lying can do, there is no better example than the fractured state of our country. This is a frightening time in our nation's history, as so many of us struggle to find the truth.

Some politicians have been considered pathological liars, which is not something you see every day. This means they lie about almost everything, without any remorse or guilt. In fact, their lies are so unabashed and frequent that in some cases they honestly believe they are telling the truth. Lying is an addiction for them, but not in the traditional way we have established. The psychological illness of a pathological liar is much more pronounced than the dysfunctional patterns most of us experience. Those of us who aren't pathological liars don't lie all the time, about everything. We may stretch the truth, but we generally do not seek to intentionally mislead.

Exaggeration is another way people play with the truth, although the intent may be to entertain rather than deceive. You probably know someone who loves to exaggerate. For me, it was my brother. He could spin a yarn with the best of them. So many times he would sit in our dimly lit kitchen and recount a story that pushed the bounds of reality. He was known for it, and it was one of his most celebrated character traits. His friends clamored for tales of his youth, knowing full well that with each version, new and exciting details would be added. His confidence and exuberance overwhelmed any desire to correct him, as his listeners became lost in the color of his imagination. So, he received a hall pass for his role of storyteller. But exaggeration, even when appreciated, is a form of duplicity, and if it is well received, it may become addictive.

So, why do people exaggerate? Well, there is the creative aspect of fictionalizing anecdotes for the purpose of entertainment, like my brother—a fairly benign practice, more playful than destructive. But not all of us are bards, and our tendency to aggrandize stems from a different place. It may be a fear-based, ego-driven response to the limiting belief that we are not good enough. Unfortunately, this common anxiety has no basis in reality, but we live in a competitive society. We tend to view the world through a prism of comparison; if we suspect that the lives of others are more desirable, we may embellish our own circumstances. If we are naturally introverted, we long to be loquacious, believing our shyness makes us inadequate. If we are extroverted, we crave to be the center of attention, as if the adoration of others will in some way soothe our unease. Even when we complain, people may try to one-up us with their own tales of woe. All such modification is simply a confirmation of one of our most basic fears: that others are better than us.

Exaggeration is spawned by dissatisfaction. Those who exaggerate frequently are consumed by obsessive thoughts of unremarkable normalcy. It is a defense mechanism that protects them from an admission of their own inadequacy. And it fits neatly into our working definition of addiction—obsessive thoughts followed by compulsive actions. The obsessive thoughts spring from low self-esteem mixed with a desire to be loved. The compulsive action is the expansion of the truth. So what is the harm of a little hyperbole? Why is this a big deal if we hear it all the time, even from people we love? It may be a slippery slope. Perhaps you bend the truth slightly at first—if the result is increased popularity, validation, and interest from others, it may be hard not to keep bending, or bend it further. This is when we may become caught in an addictive cycle.

The counterpoint to exaggeration is humility—a concept that is widely misunderstood. Humility is an innate quality that we all possess, but it isn't often that we see it in action. It is an attitude of complete nonjudgment, making it elusive to many, as a main component of the ego is to judge others. Humility is the understanding that we are all of equal stature; no one is above or beneath anyone else. It is an all-inclusive, nondiscriminatory attitude that considers all genders, races, creeds, religions, and nationalities with equal respect. Being humble does not mean that you must agree with all the beliefs of others, only that you approach them with curiosity and acceptance. Individuals with humility do not recoil from criticism, as it has no bearing on their sense of themselves. Similarly, humble people are not affected by praise and validation, as they know there is a difference between confidence and pride and they are in a constant state of self-affirmation.

Think of some people you've looked down upon in the past (perhaps you still do) and imagine your negative thoughts toward them dissolving—how freeing this would be. A cornerstone of humility is the practice of self-love. Sometimes, my patients refer to a part of themselves they dislike—*I hate my laugh* or *I am cursed by my addiction*. I offer them an alternative perspective, one of tolerance and nonjudgment. I ask them what it would feel like to love all their parts equally, even the unwanted ones, even the ones they lie about to others, and themselves. I let them know that it was through loving my addiction that I finally understood it better. I formed a relationship with my addiction, instead of repressing and dismissing it. I wrapped my arms around it, instead of turning my back on it, and this was all the attention it needed to calm down. This allowed the ego to put down its defenses. Treating your entire being, warts and all, with kindness will ultimately help to remove the roadblocks of ego.

When we dabble in falsehoods and controvert one of our core values, we are the ones who suffer. Although lies may give us an immediate escape from admitting something uncomfortable, there are destructive ramifications that will appear down the road. Even if we are lying for noble intentions—the ego does not want you or others to feel hurt—the avoidance of pain creates more, as it perpetually pushes us to lie in order to escape the psychological pain created by lying. We are still defying a fundamental cornerstone of our belief system, and there are consequences for this—problematic ones. The act of deception contradicts your authentic self. You were born of truth, and in the depths of your psyche, you remain rooted in this principle—we all do. Each time you lie, you are creating a small traumatic fissure in your psyche. These tears allow the entry of negative emotions such as anxiety, depression, and anger. Lies aren't just hard to keep straight; they also take their toll on your emotional stability and decimate your self-esteem. These distressing feelings may remain dormant at first but will soon rise to the surface, into consciousness. You may be tormented by troubling thoughts, pessimism, sadness, and frustration. Once again, the remedy comes from the soul.

To be more honest, we must align with the soul rather than the ego. The soul is completely and rigorously honest. In fact, the soul cannot fully comprehend the essence of a lie, as it has never engaged with one. But the soul does bear witness to all the dishonesty that emerges from the ego mind. When we lie, we may be unable to hear the voice of our soul over the storm of insecurity and self-doubt. But even in these moments, a small fraction of the soul's wisdom may be felt in our gut—we know that we are off track. Have you ever felt that little uncomfortable twinge as you tell a lie? As if a tiny angel was tapping on your shoulder, trying to tell you something? That is your soul alerting you that whatever choice you just made might be one you'll regret.

If our lie is the result of an ego on the defense, perhaps we harbor a belief about ourselves that is too painful to admit. As we have discussed earlier, our belief system is established mainly by unprocessed traumatic experiences from childhood. It is often difficult to make the link between the causal incident and the harmful belief—we have blocked it out or repressed it. This is another way the soul can be helpful. Our souls never forget anything and hold an exact road map of our trauma and how it has affected us. And they want nothing more than to share the details with you in one of their many languages.

We all dream every night, regardless if we remember them or not. Dream life is an active part of your sleep process. Most of us have been told that dreams are not real, that they are a figment of our imagination. I beg to differ. I believe that dreams are intentional, meaningful, and have a distinct message for each one of us. Carl Jung analyzed over twenty thousand dreams in his lifetime and believed that they were the most essential way through which to understand the very inception of our delicate emotions. He wrote, "The dream is a little hidden door in the innermost secret recesses of the soul, opening into that cosmic night which was psyche long before there was any ego-consciousness."[31] The soul's mission, shared through the images in your dreams, is to foster healing through the process of revelation and self-discovery. Unfortunately, most of us are puzzled by our dreams and have little success deciphering their meaning. We are not taught the language of dreams in school, and, in my opinion, dream books can be filled with misinformation, so I don't recommend them. I will give you a crash course in Jungian dream interpretation right now. I promise you, it's easy.

The language of dreams does not come in the form of spoken words. It is derived mainly from images, symbols, metaphors, and archetypes. Our dreams are filled with images, places, artifacts, and people that are all symbolic, not literal. So, if you dream about a particular person or place, you are not dreaming about them specifically, but what they represent. In dreams, all

---

31 Jung, C. G. *Civilization in Transition*. United Kingdom: Taylor & Francis, 2014, 144.

the people you encounter represent aspects of yourself. They constitute your character traits, attributes, and emotions. If the American modernist painter Georgia O'Keeffe visits your dream, you are being shown your artistic nature—you get the picture. A depth psychological approach to dream analysis would offer that the soul is shown as masculine for women and feminine for men. When a woman dreams about a man who is familiar and captivating, she is dreaming about her soul. Conversely, when a man dreams about a familiar, intriguing woman, this also marks the presence of soul.[32] These are wonderful dreams to have, as your soul is making you aware that it is actively presiding over your dream experience.

When you wake up from a dream, it is vital to pay attention. I recommend buying a dream notebook that you keep on your bedside table with a pencil ready to go. Upon awakening, jot down a few of the images you remember as well as the general theme and action of the dream. I'll give you an example. *I was sitting in a red rowboat on the lake in Central Park with my father, who looked much younger. He passed me a Brady Bunch lunch box and told me we had to get to shore before we were arrested. I rowed and rowed, but the boat wouldn't move. I heard police sirens in the background. I was scared.*

---

32 Fordham, Michael, Jung, C. G., Read, Herbert, Adler, Gerhard. *Collected Works of C. G. Jung, Volume 9 (Part 2): Aion: Researches Into the Phenomenology of the Self.* United Kingdom: Princeton University Press, 1953, 16.

In this dream I would focus on the rowboat, the lake in Central Park, the lunch box, your younger father, and the police. What do these images mean to you? Your young father and the lunch box refer to an earlier time in your life. What qualities do you possess that you share with your father? Strength? Anxiety? Resourcefulness? Was there an incident in your childhood that involved a lake or water? Do the police represent punishment? Safety? For the people in your dream—what qualities do you share with them? How did their presence in the dream make you feel? For the places—was there a notable incident in your past that occurred in a similar setting? How did you feel when you were there in the dream? What does that moment in your life symbolize?

These are the questions you want to ask when piecing together a dream. You must play detective as the soul is offering you clues. Remember, these images are shared from the soul for your benefit—to help you heal, grow, and evolve psychologically. Often we must revisit old wounds, traumatic moments, and confusing experiences in our dreams so that we may bring them into consciousness and address them as adults.

The soul offers us healing solutions in our dreams that are both insightful and explicit. Dreams are compensatory—their purpose is to assist in the restoration of our emotional balance. Negative emotions and self-destructive patterns are often represented as frightening people or monsters in dreams. Addiction is usually construed in this manner and is a masculine figure for men, feminine for women. So if you are dreaming about a dark figure that is pursuing you in a frightening way, this is probably a dream about the obsessive and compulsive loop you may be trapped in. Dishonesty, as an addiction, will be represented this way—as a dark figure or ominous beast that is lurking in the shadows.

The most pertinent question about the addictive loop of dishonesty is: Why are you doing it in the first place? There are details to be gleaned from the dream that will accurately pinpoint the origins of your dishonesty. Look for an indication of the time period and location. Also, be mindful of the dream's narrative elements. Your soul is presenting these clues so that you may establish the traumatic origin stories of your lies. This trauma has led to negative and limiting beliefs about yourself that continue to impede your truthfulness.

As we have discussed earlier in the book, once you have established the origins of a harmful belief, it is necessary to revisit your younger self. Refer back to the Time Angel exercise in Chapter Six with this new guidance from your dreams. Your soul is waiting for you.

# 12 | THE FUTURE AND THE PAST

The other day on a local hiking trail, I bumped into an old friend I hadn't seen in a while. Since I'm a psychologist, it seems that people, regardless of my relationship to them, like to share their stories with me. Something was obviously bothering my friend. They had made a bad decision and had lied to their partner about a promotion that they didn't get, and the partner found out the truth a few days later. They told me they had not slept well for a week and that they kept obsessing about the moment they felt compelled to mislead their partner. I watched them amble down the trail with their head shaking, muttering to themself. Poor fellow. I had heard it all before—perhaps not with these exact details, but the archetypal tale of regret and the

159

resulting distractions it caused. There, on the hiking trail, in the midst of mountainous splendor, my friend was consumed by the past.

You may have heard some variation of the saying "If you have one foot in the past and one foot in the future, you're pissing on the present." I could not agree more. Most of us struggle to remain present in our daily lives. We daydream about future events that may influence the trajectory of our life and career. We ruminate about moments in the past that have impacted our character and sense of self. In some instances, reflecting upon our bygones and fantasizing about things to come fill us with a sense of accomplishment and hope, but this is not as common as we'd like. Much of the time, our thoughts drift into the darkness of the past and uncertainty about the future. Herein lies the trouble. Our emotional state is easily altered by unsettling memories and fear of the unknown, and this prevents us from enjoying the moment we're in. As we stumble through our regrets and fixate on moments yet to come, we walk past beautiful architecture, interesting people, and captivating elements in nature without even noticing them. The ego has usurped our natural ability to enjoy the sanctity of the moment in which we are living. This is not the way of the soul.

I know how overwhelming this feeling can be. I once had too much to drink and yelled at a friend for taking away my car keys. I said terrible, combative things. Of course, when I woke up the next morning, I was filled with shame. I was embarrassed and disappointed with myself, and these feelings lasted for quite some time. Years later, recalling the incident made me cower with chagrin. I apologized profusely, but I still couldn't shake the agony of my guilt. I felt like a failure who had betrayed my core values. Well, there was the alcohol, for one, that inhibited my better judgment, but it was more than that. The stain of my egocentricity would not wash away. I supposed I was doomed from the start, as I had drifted so far away from my soul that it was no longer visible. I lived this way for much of my life.

Both my friend on the hike and I were consumed by the mistakes we had made and unable to move past them. We were stuck in the mire of guilt—a toxic place. You've likely seen it before—a friend or family member remains scarred by their past behavior whether they want to speak about it or not. As human beings, we make mistakes all the time. We lie, we cheat and blame others, we unleash torrents of anger upon them. When confronted by certain complicated situations, we make inappropriate choices that hurt others. It is not in our nature to behave this way, but our self-centered protective measures lead us astray, and most of us then feel remorse. We think back to that defining moment and wish we had responded differently. Or perhaps we are the victim in a scenario, rather than the perpetrator, and we wish someone had not hurt us. We run over the scenario in our mind and imagine a more favorable outcome. But either way, the truth is our hands are tied—the infraction is cemented in time and can't be undone. This is where the suffering begins.

So, why do we get so stuck? Why can't we move on and release ourselves from an incident's prolonged psychological impact? When we find ourselves incapable of letting the past go, we are caught in a cycle of addiction. We obsess over the past harm, whether done by us or to us. Our compulsion is demonstrated through the negative emotions we attach to the past experiences—shame, guilt, embarrassment, anger, and resentment. Our obsessive thoughts compel us to feel victimized or guilty. As we will see, our preoccupation with the future also fits into our working definition of addiction, as our obsessive thoughts about the unknown keep us in the grip of compulsive worrying.

It is always ego that beckons us to live in the past. The soul has no truck with it, none at all. In fact, the soul does not reference time in a linear way. The past, future, and present merge together in the soul's consciousness. The soul recognizes your past simply as energy that combines with the present, collective energy that creates your humanity. The soul's understanding of time is far more advanced than that of our mortal construct, and therefore the soul does not dwell on anything that has already occurred. Remember, the soul's intention is to foster your ability to actualize as the best version of yourself. It is not deterred or dissuaded by the will of the ego and has nothing but compassion for your less evolved elements. The soul comprehends the complexities of being human and remains our most stalwart companion, especially when we stumble and fall. This is when we need our soul the most. It will always roll up its sleeves and pull us from the depths of our own depravity.

The soul forgives us for being human—and all that comes with it. It lays out the path to break free from self-judgment and self-hatred. The soul encourages you to embrace yourself and adopt an attitude of sufferance. It asks that you stop taking yourself so seriously and, instead, take accountability for your many ego-based transgressions with a lightness of heart. Let the child in you emerge—the child who stays in the present, always. This child intuitively knows how to release themselves from the guilt of culpability. This does not absolve you from your mistakes but allows you to acknowledge them without humiliation. We discussed how to forgive ourselves with affirmations in Chapter Eight. I advocate that you do the exercise in Chapter Eight every morning. It is part of my spiritual practice and has transformed my opinion of myself. Align with the soul and you will leave the past in its rightful place: the rearview mirror.

When you adopt an attitude of listening, not speaking, the noise inside your mind diminishes and allows you to be in the moment. Listening is hard (believe me, I do it for a living) and requires patience, attentiveness, and empathy—all qualities of the soul. Try this on for size.

### Exercise
*One day this week, you are going to be a listener and not a talker. For a three-hour period on any day you choose, you are only going to speak when asked a direct question. Try to really hear what is being asked of you.*

*Focus on the person asking and look them in the eye when you respond. Be present and in the moment of the discussion. And then, keep quiet. Developing your listening skills is an important way to rebalance the ego and restore its healthy function.*

When we are the victim, it is not humiliation or guilt that has us stuck. Victim consciousness is an archetypal pattern that is a likely cause of emotional stagnation, as it is an ego-attached state. We are enraged that we have been treated unfairly, disrespected, ignored, or dismissed. We blame others for our circumstances and wallow in self-pity. Victimhood can be the result of a wide range of experiences, from microaggressions to horrific abuse and neglect. Whatever has happened to you, know that you do not have to remain in victim consciousness. This state shackles the mind and limits its ability to expand. Traumatic events in our past need to be excavated, treated, and healed, but they should not inhibit your ability to evolve; they are best addressed alongside a change in perception. Instead of considering yourself a victim, reassess the situation and recall your heroism and bravery.

No one has the ability to remove your dignity. Your soul wants you to forgive the perpetrators of the offense so that you may be free. It is through the soul's forgiveness of others that you will release the anguish of the past. No one can do it for you. Cast aside the ego's false narrative that dismisses forgiveness as weakness. Remember, your soul's foundation is built on the principles of compassion and amnesty. When you forgive others, even the unfortunates who participated in your suffering, you are complying with the will of the soul. This will allow you to forget the past and revel in the present. Here is an affirmation that will help you with this. Upon awakening, repeat these words three times.

> *To all those who have ever done me wrong, I forgive you.*
> *Nothing you have done has changed my ability to love.*
> *I am not a victim.*
> *I am a hero.*
> *I forgive you for the darkness in your heart.*
> *I forgive you for your thoughtless words and careless deeds.*
> *I no longer think of you in anger.*
> *I no longer live in the past.*
> *Today, I have arrived in the present moment of my life.*

The future is a mystery. If only we had a crystal ball to guide us through the unknown territory that lies ahead. We spend plenty of time pondering what lurks around the corner, but quite often, we are plain wrong. And yet, if our daydreams of what's to come are positive, optimistic, and expansive, this is actually a beneficial pastime. It's known as *manifesting*—projecting desired accomplishments into the universe through hopeful images in the mind. Some people swear by it and have experienced incredible results. The soul wants you to dream big, so this practice is congruent with the will of the soul.

### Exercise

*Close your eyes and imagine something that you really want. Perhaps it is a promotion or a romantic partner or a house in the mountains. Be specific. See yourself sitting in your boss's office as they offer you the new job. Watch yourself opening the door to your new home. What color is it? What does the garden look like? Witness yourself on a date with your dream partner. Manifesting is creating an image in your mind and believing that it is possible. Think of these images often, whenever you can. Cut out images from a magazine and tack them onto your bulletin board or make a screen saver with the pictures that coincide with your dreams. The more you believe, the better chance these things will come into your life. They may take a while, but be patient—if you place your positive energy in the direction of these elements, they are likely to come true.*

But most of us don't engage in manifesting. The most prevalent way that most of us see the future is through the lens of fear. We obsess about the possibility of failure, not success. There is something about the unknown that frightens us. Tomorrow could bring an earthquake, a fire—a catastrophe. We think about the worst-case scenario, especially when we receive unsettling news. A pain in our stomach can lead to hours on the internet with Dr. Google until we are convinced we have a terminal disease. Say we're asked to give a speech at work. Alarm bells go off. We fantasize about freezing up at the podium and making a fool of ourselves, which will surely lead to a demotion or even unemployment. We ruminate about the shame we will feel when everyone discovers our incompetence. There is no bottom to the rabbit hole our mind is capable of spiraling down when we are saddled by anxiety and paranoia. When things don't turn out as badly as we imagine, we scold ourselves for the time wasted, vowing to never let it happen again. But soon, faced once more with unease and uncertainty, we fall prey to catastrophic thinking.

Fear, like addiction, is simply energy. Fear of the future is an ego-based narrative that slips into our psyche through the cracks made by past experience. It doesn't belong to us and is not our natural way of being. Rather, it comes and goes according to the circumstances we are confronted with. Sometimes we can keep that fear from overwhelming us, remembering that we are strong and capable. But other times, the fear is strong. Our thoughts become jumbled, unbalanced, and irrational as adrenaline rushes through our veins. There are many ways to calm this fear surge, such as the breathing exercise in Chapter Ten or listening to the voice of the soul to replace limiting beliefs with its narrative of love, as outlined in Chapter One's exercise.

There is also a simple and more immediate method I recommend to help you stay present. This exercise will remove you from the powerful cycle of obsessive thoughts and compulsive emotions. When you find yourself agonizing over the past or troubled by the future, try this out.

## Exercise

*Find a place to sit outside in direct sunlight. If you are indoors, find a bright place next to a lamp or under a bright light. Turn your hand over and look closely at your palm. There are hundreds of tiny wrinkles that form a distinct pattern over the contours of your skin. These are your DNA strands appearing in the flesh. No one but you has this exact imprint, and nobody ever will. Get to know these physiological markers by inspecting them with love. Count how many grooves there are clustered together and trace the concentric lines as they intersect with the larger wrinkles on your hands. I guarantee you are now fully present. Now, if you are able to, look up at the sky and take notice of one beautiful element in nature. Find a tree or a leaf or a cloud. Stare at it awhile. What do you like about it?*

*Whenever you find yourself in the midst of obsessive thinking, repeat this exercise.*

## Synchronicity

One of the most playful expressions of the soul is through the mysterious occurrence of synchronicity. Carl Jung spent years researching the connection between the inner world of thought and emotion and the outer world of tangible form. In many cases, there was a direct link between the two that was unmistakable and utterly without scientific explanation. Jung wrote, "Synchronicity is the coming together of inner and outer events in a way that cannot be explained by cause and effect and that is meaningful to the observer."[33] So, according to Jung, these serendipitous happenings have no rational explanation. Perhaps you may have experienced them? Something happens to you at just the right moment—when you need it most. You think about an old friend you haven't seen in years, and at that exact moment, they call you; you go from feeling alone to connected in a matter of seconds. In the shower you hum a tune from an old, obscure playlist in college, and while you're driving to work, the same song pops on the radio. You turn it up and sing along, your spirit renewed. We wonder who is intervening in our lives at this very moment—it seems to be someone who cares, obviously. Synchronicities immediately bring us back to the present and quiet our self-centered, ego-based thoughts with the recognition that something extraordinary is happening.

The soul is intentional about when to send us these extraordinary messages. Usually, they appear when we are distracted by the past or overwhelmed by thoughts of the future. Synchronicities are designed to bring our feet back to the ground so we become aware of what's right in front of us. If we ponder something

---

33  Jung, C. G. *Synchronicity: An Acausal Connecting Principle.* United Kingdom: Taylor & Francis, 2013, 41.

and then it manifests, we are forced to confront the notion that we are not alone in the universe. Our soul is extending its collaborative energy to draw something into the forefront of our attention. Jung's hypothesis of a synchronistic world was a diverse mixture of occurrences in the tangible world forming a delicate balance with fragments of the unknown, each complementing the others in the realms of psyche and matter. In this conception, a relationship exists between what is proven and what is inexplicable. Jung believed that synchronistic moments were elements of a universal, archetypal pattern that help people heal and grow. He surmised that archetypes are brought into consciousness as purposeful and compounding acts of the soul.

When we are overcome with emotional distress, our soul steps in. When we are lost in the misdeeds of our past and struggling in the angst of the future, synchronicities arrive at our doorstep. When our limiting beliefs become a torrential downpour, our soul opens the umbrella. If you open your mind and look around, you will start to find synchronicities everywhere. What you previously would have shrugged off as a random coincidence will look far more complex. There are no coincidences. These occurrences are meant to help us pause and restore faith in ourselves. Fashioned in the deepest place of love in our psyche, synchronicities are the lighthouses that guide us to shore in the darkness of night. They allow us to glimpse that psychological pain will end. And it always does.

## Déjà Vu

Have you ever been in a specific situation and sworn that you had been there before—but when? How? You have a sense that you have lived this moment previously—the sounds, the location, and the conversation are mysteriously familiar, but you cannot place them. This is the phenomenon of déjà vu. When these unexplainable moments arrive in our consciousness, there is usually a pause, a recognition of the event, and a quick dismissal that our mind is playing tricks on us. Well, in these moments, it is not your cognitive function that is leading the way—quite the contrary.

A déjà vu is another message from the soul designed to bring you into the present moment. The soul is asking you to pay attention and letting you know that you are on the right path. In actuality, you *have* experienced these instances before. You have dreamed them, and remember, the soul is the architect of your dream life. The soul has shown you this moment in your unconscious sleep state long before it actually transpires in the tangible world. In dreams, it is giving you a glimpse of what's to come—a preview of your future. Do not dismiss a déjà vu as a figment of your imagination. Recognize that it is intentional and created by the soul. In these well-orchestrated seconds—mere blips in time, considering the vastness of human experience—you are being shown information that is contrary to any logic-seeking deductions of the ego. As I mentioned, in the soul's world, time is not linear, and therefore the past and future often merge together in the present. This is the case with a déjà vu. When you experience these rare occurrences, take notice of whom you are with and what is being said. Reflect on the details of the situation. Ponder the importance of this poignant intervention from the soul. Stay with it awhile and accept the confirmation that you are in the right place at the right time. This recognition will keep you right here, right now, in the present.

# AFTERWORD
## KEEPING IN TOUCH: SOUL EDITION

My journey of rediscovering and reconnecting with my soul happened over the course of fifteen years. Thanks to my daily practice of the exercises shared in this book, I manage to live (mostly) in alignment with it. I can quickly identify the creep of the ego well before the energy of addiction flows in, and I use the tools in this book to deflect that flow. I work every day to stay in good touch with my soul. Noticing and then interrupting your obsessive thinking and compulsive action loop require practice, but once you master these skills, you too will be free from addiction. Your soul doesn't just hope you can do it; your soul knows you can.

# ACKNOWLEDGMENTS

To all those friends who have stood in my corner, even in the darkest hours. Ted Wiard, Mike Nasatir, Bob Timmons, Jon Sidel, Gary Kohn, Donal Ward, Shannon Freedle, Muffy Stout, Anthony Stout, Craig Stout, Antonia Stout, Julie Stout, Lyn Stout, Marcus Stout, Deborah McKinlay, Jonathan Marc Sherman, Alexandra Shiva, Alessandro Nivola, Adam Moreno, Seth Herzog, Billy Crudup, Nick Paumgarten, Richard DuPont, Matthew Warren, Don Pillsbury, Cristina Cuomo, Fernanda Niven, Emma Pilkington Goergen, Craig Borten, Katherine Kendall, Kay Kendall, Syd Butler, Gavin Johnston, Katherine Kousi, Polo Bizot, Judy Bizot, Tara Fisher, Tasmin Fisher, Caroline Cass, Jennifer Franchina, Alessandra Franchina, Deborah

175

Gillette, Gene Baro, Lillie B. Johnson, Feli Orinion, Stevie Lowe, Christine Markatos, Sarah Watson, Hardi Ophels, Jim Garavente, Luke McDunough, Kevin Saleeby, Carlton Prickett, Terry Brown, Will Stubbs, Bob Myerson, Trevor Groth, Chris Fisher, Brendon Blake, Peter Dinklage, Jason Blum, Jesse and Nick Lee, Ingrid Jeppson, John Jeppson, Bree Jeppson, Eric and Nancy Jeppson, Rory and Adeline Rooney, Coley Laffoon, Nicholas Fisher, Silas Mitchell, Helen Stubbs, Alex Paine, Dave Caulkins, John Trevor, Ellen Najjar, Valerie Smith, Devon Smith, Cathy Bando, Bruce Duffy, Susan Pola, Lent Howard, Hugh Allen, Kevin McDonnell, Dave Crommwell, Alex Buffon, Bill Slover, Steve Szoradi, Andrew Moe, David Ferris, Jon Smith, Diego Winegardner, Marlon Richards, the Swanhaus brothers, Lisa LoCicero, Jennifer Keohane, Sara Daley, Wendy Hoopes, Becky and Michael McDonald, Tom Lennon, Lane Heymont, Greg Hannley, Will McCormack, Sarah Brokaw, Carole Radziwill, Stephanie Laska, Barbara Stamis, Smith Publicity, PubVendo, Julie Miesionczek, and the folks at *Goop*, especially Gwyneth Paltrow. I am indebted to all of you. You helped me get here . . .